The
Parentalk
Guide to
Being a Dad

The
Parenalk
Guide to
Being a Dad

Peter Meadows

Series Editor: Steve Chalke

Illustrated by John Byrne

Hodder & Stoughton
LONDON SYDNEY AUCKLAND

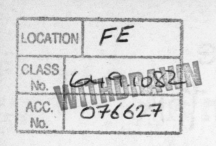
Copyright © 2000 by Parentalk
Illustrations copyright © 2000 by John Byrne

First published in Great Britain in 2000

The right of Peter Meadows to be identified as the Author of
the Work has been asserted by him in accordance with
the Copyright, Designs and Patents Act 1988.

10 9 8 7 6 5 4 3

British Library Cataloguing in Publication Data
A record for this book is available from the British Library

ISBN 0 340 75655 1

Typeset by Avon Dataset Ltd, Bidford-on-Avon, Warks

Printed and bound in Great Britain by
Clays Ltd, St Ives plc

Hodder and Stoughton
A Division of Hodder Headline Ltd
338 Euston Road
London NW1 3BH

Contents

Acknowledgements

My thanks in respect of this book go in three directions:

- To Mavis Beacon, my invaluable touch-typing tutor, who built my self-esteem as she prodded me forward.
- To my five great kids – Kristen, Joel, Aran, Zac and Xanna – who have taught me so much.
- To Rosemary – my wife, partner, friend, lover and encourager – by far the best 'dad' my kids could possibly have.

Introduction

If only being a dad was like owning a VCR. The experience would then come complete with a pause button – to use while you work out what to do next. A rewind control – to have another go. And an erase facility – to remove all evidence of failure.

Even better, how about a remote control and an automatic timer – so you're always able to make whatever you want happen to order?

Dream on. Life's not like that. Nor is being a dad. And, unlike with the VCR, no advice from a four-year-old techno-expert is going to do you any good at all.

So here you are reaching out for help. Or are you?

More likely someone has thrust this book at you with a heavy 'read this – it will do you good' attitude. I know, because in truth men have very little interest in what it means to be a dad. If you are a rare exception – congratulations.

You can tell how switched off men are on the issue of parenting by research on the subject that took place a couple of years ago. It was not the outcome of this major study that is revealing but the process itself.

The research company worked their butts off to create a number of balanced discussion groups in terms of age, social background and gender. But none of the men turned up – at

1

best, sending their partner instead.

The researchers had another go. This time inviting only men – and even offering the inducement of money to get them there. The outcome? Just as bad!

Why? Perhaps it's down to that great typically male attitude of 'What's in it for me?' If the answer is 'Not a lot' then why bother?

So let me promise you that this little book does have something for you – in terms of fulfilment, reduced haste and an enhanced ability to survive.

Or course, not everything is for you right now. No individual – at one and the same time – can be an expectant dad, a new dad, a schooldays dad, an adolescent offspring dad, a single dad, a dad at a distance or whatever. But there's more than enough here to meet your needs now and in the future. So keep it handy. Along with your emergency phone number for the plumber and your get-out-of-jail-free card.

Who am I to talk? If the under-eighteen years of my five children were laid end to end I'd have been a dad for ninety years. That has certainly taught me something – at times painfully. And where my experience is a little thin I've grabbed the insights of those who have been where I have not.

So, be you a willing reader or not, let's go.

And remember, be nice to your children – they are those who will choose your retirement home.

A Case of Mistaken Identity?

Me – a Dad?

It was one of the most profound and life-changing experiences ever to have come my way. From the hospital car park I could see the second-storey window behind which my first-born and his mother, Rosemary, were safely tucked up. The eight-hour labour – complete with a swooping blackbird in the delivery room – was recent history. Now the proud dad was back out in the real world – which was when it happened.

I slipped into the driver's seat of my car, as I had a thousand times before. Yet this time it was all so different. Here I was constantly and carefully checking and rechecking my seat belt. And driving with a care and caution never before in my repertoire. The responsibility of fatherhood had landed squarely on my somewhat broad shoulders. It was so real I could almost touch it.

From this moment on, I was responsible for a new life, a new relationship and a new future. My actions and decisions now carried a new significance, with implications not only for me but two other people. The buck stopped here. A page – a whole chapter even – had been turned in an instant. The responsibility which was now mine felt simply and awesomely overwhelming.

And all because I was now a dad.

No one warned me I would feel this way. There was a lot else they had left me ignorant of, too. Like projectile vomiting, the tantrums of terrible twos, the impact of chewing gum on hair and the terror of school open evenings. As a dad yourself you are somewhere on that journey – or, as an expectant one, are on its threshold. But what exactly *is* a dad?

You Are Not a Mum

The difference between mums and dads is more profound than them having differing biological functions and plumbing. In fact, at the time in history when society would have us believe both genders have identical skills and abilities, science is beginning to demonstrate the opposite. There are basic differences in the way the sexes think and behave – which are more profound than the much quoted 'women can't read maps and men can't listen'. Or the social phenomenon that women go to the loo in pairs and men singularly.

Women Have Abilities All Their Own

Men and women are certainly equal. But they are not identical – as contemporary research into the human brain reveals. For example, it's claimed, a woman's brain is pro- grammed to hear and respond to a child's cry at night – while a man tends to dream on in ignorance.

'Really, darling? Four times in the night?' I remember saying in all innocence on countless occasions. 'Sorry, didn't hear a thing. And you know I'd have done my bit if I had.'

For you the difference in nature may mean a better night's sleep – although something of an earful in the morning and the potential of resentment. Far better is to recognise that mothers are different and plan accordingly. You could:

- Agree that your partner has permission to wake you to take your turn.
- Sleep close to the scene of the crime so as to be quick off the mark.

Experiments also show mothers can read the signals of hunger, pain, wind and tiredness just from a ten-second silent film clip of their child. Fathers on the other hand, who watched the same footage, remained basically clueless.[1]

The female ear can also detect subtle shifts in voice-tone and pitch in later life which signal something is emotionally wrong – while men charge on into the day in sweet oblivion. This means you are never going to be as observant or intuitive as your child's mother so far as the needs of your offspring are concerned.

'I want a drink of water and I want it now,' had yelled our

four-year-old Zachary. 'And it must be in a cup. It must, it must, it must.'

To me this was no more than an over-tired infant behaving unreasonably. Rosemary's intuitive antenna gave her far greater insight. She probed further – to discover the water was not for drinking at all, but for some urgent fire-fighting. Left to his own devices, and with matches that should have been well out of reach, Zachary had started a fire – now roaring away under the stairs and needing to be extinguished.

You will do well to learn to take notice of the distinct abilities of your partner in the realm of hearing and intuitive recognition. And to remember these attributes will not dim with the aging of your child. They are invaluable from birth to teenage years and at all stops in between.

With this in mind make sure you:

- Don't belittle your partner's voice of concern just because you may be blind to the signals that, to her, are as clear as an oil slick on an iceberg.
- Accept that you need help in being aware of the personal needs and concerns of your child, rather than insisting that you know best.

 Top Tip: Learn to trust the special ability a mother has for spotting what's wrong.

You Have Distinct Roles

Without going into stereotype overdrive, men and women also operate differently – with each having a unique contribution to make to the role of parenting. Throughout history the male has tended to be the provider and protector and the female the nurturer and carer. This has been more than simply a useful way to define roles. It springs from something deep within us.

In today's society such role models are becoming increasingly blended and often for the good. But in the main, the distinctives are worth hanging on to because, by doing so, you will play to your strengths and your partner will play to hers.

Of course, there will be times when your motherly instinct and abilities have to come to the fore. From night feeds to filling in when mum's missing or she's simply had enough. And the opposite will be true for her.

Your strengths are likely to include stamina, decision-making, accepting responsibility and objective reasoning. They are by no means your exclusive domain, but they are likely to be where *you* will do your best. So when the phone call came with the news that Zac was in hospital sixty miles away with a broken arm – thanks to some daft activity on a church youth outing – it was never in doubt that I would make the journey and sleep on the floor next to him. I knew my place.

In the same way, arriving at a holiday mobile home in France, I could foresee endless arguments about who would do what in the way of chores, with Rosemary ending up with two week's worth of short straws. My logical male mind lurched into action – and a rota was produced. It was not much more complicated than the average 'who makes the coffee' office rota. But it worked a treat. No one argued and Rosemary's name was not on it!

You Are Not Yesterday's Dad

Despite what I have said about male and female roles, the world has changed in just two generations. My dad worked all hours and came home to a meal on the table or there would have been trouble. He provided and protected, did the jobs about the house and that was that. Meanwhile, I had a mother who cleaned, sewed, cooked and brought up the children – with the exception of the 'you wait until your father comes home' routine.

That has all changed – yet, for some and maybe you – the shadow of yesterday can still fall over today's parenting. Often this can come from parents or grandparents – yours or hers – who see the current blending of roles as a sign of a lack of masculinity or being under the thumb.

Never having seen my dad change a nappy, rustle up a meal or iron a shirt was a barrier to me sharing the load in a relationship that demanded a fairer share of the chores and responsibilities. 'What would he think?' my subconscious mind would rumble. Or what if someone came to the door while I had a vacuum cleaner on the growl?

No matter how it was for you as a child, or what voices prompt you from the wings, it's vital to define manhood and fatherhood in ways other than avoiding traditional 'woman's work' that includes everything from household chores to bath time to school open evenings.

 Top Tip: Ask yourself, am I doing my share of the workload?

You Are Not Superdad

You have seen those performers in a circus who spin plates on the end of poles. They rush about like demented chickens from one pole to another in order to keep the show on the road. By the end of the act they have about thirty plates on the go as the audience breaks into breathless applause.

Life for a parent can be like that – although the applause tends to be somewhat muted. But remember, after ten minutes the man with the plates takes a bow, packs them up and puts them away until the next show.

Be realistic. You can't be everywhere at once with an endless supply of boundless energy. There is a limit to the number of plates you can spin and for how long. As a dad you need to pace yourself – and to make sure your partner does the same.

While you are in the world of coming to terms with reality, make up your mind early that you are not the fountain of all wisdom and knowledge. From the earliest of ages children believe their dad has the ability to solve everything and make everything right – even without a quick change in a phone box to emerge with his underpants over his trousers. You will be tempted to believe the same.

However, the reality is, at times, you are going to get things wrong – spectacularly. Remember, no users manual was supplied. There is no free-phone helpdesk or the equivalent of Microsoft's Office Assistant to call on for wisdom at the drop of a tantrum or moment of crisis. Fifty-fifty and ask the audience are not options. And there will not always be a friend to phone even if they have the right answer.

When caught between a rock and a hard place all you have to offer is your best shot. And it won't always be on target. 'Sorry, son,' I have found myself saying on more occasions than I can remember. 'I've never before had a child your age with this situation to deal with. Next time I'll hope to do better.'

13

Top Tip: Be realistic about what you can cope with and your ability to solve every problem.

It's Tough Out There

Some Things Come with the Territory

Being a Dad Involves a Fight

It is not only hard being a dad, it can be even harder getting the right to fulfil the role of a dad. Parenting has for so long equalled 'mothering', so if you want to genuinely grab hold of what it means to be a dad in the fullest, life-enriching sense, then that's what you'll have to do – grab.

If not, it will all too easily become your lot to be an observer rather than a participator. A spectator rather than a player. It's seldom the mum's fault that this happens – it's just that the past world, where dads were fathers in a very different sense, still casts its shadow. Fathers went to war, dug the allotment, worked all hours – and left being a parent to 'her indoors'.

That's why, from day one, you are in danger of being pigeonholed as provider and carer – but not as a dad in a genuinely active sense. You'll know how true this is the first time you do something genuinely parental – feed, change or whatever. The looks and nudges say it all!

But the kick of being a dad is to *be* a dad. So don't miss it. Fight for it.

Being a Dad Involves a Steadfast Commitment

There are two huge struggles you'll face – or be facing – in making being a good dad among the highest priorities of your life. They are the level of sacrifice involved and the need for patience.

It Takes Sacrifice

First, there's the sacrifice it takes to be 'there' for your child. Making it a priority to be with your kid involves saying 'no' to things you'd love to do and to opportunities to be significant in the eyes of others.

There's a world out there – at work and at play – just waiting to tell you how important you are and to give you opportunities to demonstrate your value and potential. Meanwhile there's also the little fella who wants your time and attention – but you know giving it to him offers little opportunity to shine in the eyes of others. And this is not an occasional choice but an ongoing one.

Top Tip: *Don't underestimate the level of sacrifice it takes to 'be there' for your child.*

Second, there's also the sacrifice of giving your undivided attention – when it's so easy to bluff it and grunt. It's not enough to be there – you have to *be* there.

There is a point when I know I've been caught pretending to listen while I'm really lost in my own little world. It's when my brain finally kicks in to realise I have just heard something like, 'And then, Dad, after the penguin has danced the cancan we will shove a stick of rhubarb up your nose.'

It is a mischievous trick my kids play, and I deserve it. But it takes sacrifice to wilfully and consistently be there when I'm there. Day in and day out.

It Takes Patience

Patience, they say, is a virtue seldom found in women, never found in men, but it's the task of every dad to prove the old adage wrong. You need patience to allow your child the opportunity to do for themselves things you could do in a trice. Just think of all the valuable telly-watching and Scrabble-playing time you'd save if you tied their shoes, poured their drink, made their decisions, ended their sentences and gave them the answers to their homework.

I remember, on one occasion, the screams of delight from our child's bedroom which told us he was as happy as Larry. Whatever was going on in there did not need to be disturbed as Rosemary and I took the opportunity for an unexpected lie-in. The reason for our toddler's joy turned out to be he had turned over a small bookcase and was using the back of it as a slide – with the contents of his nappy as a lubricant! As you can imagine, his sudden burst of ingenuity had a

17

considerable impact on our store of endurance.

Your child's slow growth into maturity requires your unending patience and willingness to redo what they mess up, clean up what they spill and allow them to work it out for themselves. The easy way is unproductive in the long run. The only answer is tons of patience.

 Top Tip: *Keep your eyes open for each new experience and discovery as your child learns and grows.*

The Top Ten Things Every Child Is Waiting to Hear from Their Dad

1. You don't need to eat your sprouts if you don't want to.
2. Let's watch *Teletubbies* instead of *Match of the Day*.
3. Have you ever wondered where babies come from?
4. Haven't you done enough school work for one night?
5. Are you sure your music won't go louder?
6. I never liked that shirt anyway.
7. Isn't it time you got a tattoo?
8. I wish I had known that at your age.
9. I think the mess in your bedroom is an artistic masterpiece.
10. It's your turn for the car tonight – and I have filled the tank.

Being a Dad Means a Willingness to Adjust

There's no such thing as one-size-fits-all fathering. Kids are inherently different from each other in temperament and according to their gender. They also change over time. So just when dads think they have learned the script they can suddenly find themselves on stage in a totally different play.

 Top Tip: *There's no such thing as one-size-fits-all fathering. You have to learn to adjust.*

I've been there. Each of our children has had a very different way of responding to life – from effervescent Aran to laid back and almost horizontal Joel. After four fairly straightforward childhoods, which convinced Rosemary and I that we should think about writing a book on the joys of being a parent, came Xanna, the most difficult infant you could imagine. Had the book we had in mind actually been written we would have had to pulp the lot and issue an official apology!

Boys and Girls are Different

First for a dad to contend with is the difference between boys and girls – and I mean the less-than-obvious ones. It may surprise you but infant boys are physically more vulnerable than infant girls.

19

- At birth the male brain is significantly less mature than the female's – with a newborn girl's brain as developed as that of a six-week-old boy.
- At the age of three, boys are no good at conveying any emotion other than anger. Yet girls are even able to discuss their emotions with their mothers.
- Boys are more likely to suffer from neurological disorders and physical deformities – with more dying at birth.

The situation does not change during their growing years. For example, as they grow up:

- Boys are more likely to suffer from dyslexia and to have behavioural problems.
- Boys are four times as likely as girls to show the symptoms of hyperactivity.
- Boys generally do less well at school.
- In later life boys are more prone to depression that leads to suicide.[2]

It's claimed these problems stem from the way baby boys are treated in the first year of their life – and made worse by parents who go on to treat them with less sensitivity than girls. Recent studies show adults tend to treat boys more harshly, talk less to them and discipline them more often.

It's here that dads can so easily get it wrong. 'Don't let them see you cry, son. It's only going to need twenty stitches and a skin graft' is too close to what boys may hear when something more caring is appropriate. The 'toughen up and don't cry' attitude can damage their development at a time when they need more attention and help than girls, in order that they can develop properly.

Children Change

Adjustment also includes coming to terms with the different stages of your child's life. I can trace the journey simply by stripping the wallpaper on any of my kids' bedrooms. Furthest back are the teddy bears, next it's Thomas the Tank Engine, followed by the blue and white of the official Chelsea colours. And finally it is all topped with a subtle shade of black.

Pokémon-style, kids have this great tendency to keep evolving into something different and to do so when we least expect it. You thought you had Charmander and now it's Charmeleon and soon it will be Charizard. Can you ever keep up?

Vital to navigate are those rough and uncharted waters between dependency and independence, from the point when a child depends on knowing just how many lampposts down the street they can roam from the front gate, through to where the decisions of what, when and where are almost all their own.

On the journey between the two they will grow through a variety of stages from infant to young adult. All have distinct nuances which you will ignore at your peril because each requires a deft touch all of its own. Treat a teenager as though they are still a child and get ready to scrape the fury and indignation off the walls. Give a child the freedom that only a teenager deserves and you are storing up trouble. Both can easily happen if we don't keep our wits about us and drift into a parenting-on-automatic-pilot mode.

At each stage of development, too, your child will have a different set of emotional and relational concerns. 'Am I liked?' 'Why do I feel this way?' 'Will I cope?' 'Supposing it doesn't work out or I fail.' 'Help! What's happening to my body?' In each case, your willingness and openness to adjust will make a huge difference.

Father through the Years

4 years: My daddy can do anything.
7 years: My dad knows a lot, a whole lot.
8 years: My father doesn't quite know everything.
12 years: Oh well, naturally Father doesn't know everything.
14 years: Father? Hopelessly old-fashioned.
18 years: I know more than Dad.
21 years: Oh, that man is out of date. What did you expect?
25 years: He knows a little bit about it, but not much.
30 years: Must find out what Dad thinks about it.
35 years: A little patience; let's get Dad's idea first.
50 years: What would Dad have thought about it?
60 years: My dad knew literally everything.
65 years: I wish I could talk it over with my dad once more.

Public Domain

 Top Tip: Be sure to treat your child in ways appropriate to their age and experience.

You deserve to be pre-warned about the point at which a typical dad finds his fathering satisfaction level reaches its lowest ebb. It's during his child's adolescence – at a time when your need to adjust will be put to its greatest test.

It's the years when your child is desperately trying to find their feet in an alien world – and solving it by behaving like an alien themselves. Their value systems can charge off in an entirely different direction to your own. You feel as though your home has just become the latest member of the Holiday Inn franchise – with you as chief clerk, caterer and maid service.

And how do you show affection to a daughter who looks more like a woman than your 'little girl'? What will you say when their idea of a curfew is three hours different to yours and 'everybody but everybody' is staying over?

There are many little – yet dramatic – swings in mood and opinion that come with adolescence. A changing teen and a changing father will have a changing relationship – or else a very strained one. We must grow and adapt if we want to keep in touch.

When the time comes my best advice is hold on tight and know the time will pass. Eventually they will beam back down to Planet Earth. If nothing else, those few months before their seventeenth birthday offer real hope should they have any anticipation of ever learning to drive your car or eventually having its use. Suddenly the balance of power has shifted! You have control of the car keys and who gets to use them. When that moment comes, make the most of it!

Keep Your Eyes on the End Game

To take being a dad seriously means having your eyes on the end result from the very beginning. When finally the child flies the nest, what values and character do you want them to take with them? As management guru Steven Covey puts it, 'Begin with the end in mind.'

How do you want the crop to turn out? For some dads it's enough to survive. To get by. To do it 'good enough'. But what a difference if you capture the bigger picture. If you can see yourself not simply providing and protecting – with a little discipline and encouragement on the way and mixed with a little fun for good measure. But rather as someone shaping the whole future and destiny of an individual.

Just imagine it was not a dinky, burping, wriggling piece of humanity for which you became jointly responsible over its next eighteen years. That instead it was a few hundred thousand pounds of negotiable currency. A great, chunking mega-wad.

Think of the time and energy you'd put into making sure that bundle was invested so as to mature to its full potential. Anything else – like leaving it to chance and hoping for the best – would be foolish and unthinkable.

Top Tip: *Try never to lose sight of your long-term goal as a dad – which is to create the person you want to let loose on the world.*

Yet that young life – your offspring – also represents enormous potential. Their genes and their stars don't have it all mapped out no matter what. They have not been born into some groove of destiny that dictates what will be will be. And you have the opportunity, privilege and responsibility to help see their potential fulfilled.

The experiences and influences of your child's early years are going to shape their character, goals, skills and attitudes for a lifetime – for good or bad.

Studies tracking the outcome of the way children were parented tell us that what happens in the early years has a major impact on the way they turn out in later life. For example, watching parents argue at age seven was found to have a significant link with them arguing with their parents at sixteen and their partner at age thirty-five.[3]

But do dads matter in this life-shaping process? The answer is an unequivocal 'yes!' Boys whose fathers play an active role in their lives are less likely to get into trouble, do poorly at school or to run with the crowd. And their daughters are less likely to suffer from low self-esteem, have sex sooner than they really want to, and drop out of education.

That's not to knock the mums who were left holding the baby. It just reveals how vital being a dad is. Fathering makes a whole world of difference – for you and them.

So decide early what matters to you in terms of the end 'result'. And be sure to keep these objectives in view as you work towards the goal.

Your Long-Term Checklist

Which of these characteristics would you most like your child to leave home with?

- Self-confidence
- Social skills
- Stickability
- Honesty
- A generous spirit
- Compassion

Whatever you would like to see in your child, try to model it yourself. This will help deliver you from providing a quick fix and brushing things under the carpet. And from those instant solutions that solve the issue at the time but never confront the cause because it's easier to go for a quiet life. You know the ones I mean. The meal table explodes as, on cue, a child goes into an overload of self-will and stubborn behaviour. You are tempted to use a display of authority and power to settle the matter – without ever taking time to address the root issue and talk it out. In doing so, you have solved the problem but solved nothing. No one is wiser, only older. But, with an eye on the future, there is a better way.

Dads Can Have Stretch Marks Too

Help - I'm Going to Be a Dad

'This is it,' announced Rosemary at three in the morning. 'Sprog is on the way.' She grabbed the bag she had packed at least a millennium earlier – she is so calm and organised.

I rushed for the phone. 'My wife is pregnant, and her contractions are only two minutes apart!'

'Is this her first child?' the doctor queried.

'No, you idiot!' I screamed in reply. 'This is her husband!'

I liken coping with the first-born to being something akin to making your first aeroplane flight. You have no way of knowing if the plane is supposed to make those noises and do those things so you can't help but worry. As Kristen, our first-born, lay in the crib next to Rosemary on day two of his life, an emergency developed of epic proportions. I demanded the 'crash' team attended immediately. Finally, a nurse came running and delivered the verdict to an anxious mum and dad, 'It's only hiccups. He'll get over it.'

Start Early

If you are about to become a dad, expect no different – you're journeying into the unknown. So, from day one, go for it – seize the experience to the full. Read the books, attend the classes, hit the surf, make the hospital visits and practise giving back rubs. Go there, be there, buy the T-shirt.

It's your life. Your kid. Enjoy.

Internet Sites to Help You on Your Way

www.fathersdirect.com
Good, practical information and advice.

www.fnf.org.uk
An excellent site from Families need Fathers, particularly aimed at helping to maintain a child's relationship with both parents during and after family breakdown.

www.parentalk.co.uk
Packed with great ideas and top tips for expectant mums and dads through to grandparents.

www.b4baby.com
Ante-natal and post-natal – it's all here.

---

www.ukmums.co.uk
Don't be put off by the name, there is lots of good dad-focused stuff here.

www.bbc.co.uk/health/parenting
A valuable guide to the journey through conception to birth and beyond.

Don't hide behind a male 'I'm cool' image. Treat yourself to understanding as much as possible about the mystery and wonder of your unborn child. Looking back I wish I'd made a week-by-week chart to plot the progress as the micro-Meadows developed shape and form, heart, lungs and all the rest. Make the most of the last nights you'll get when you can be sure of unbroken sleep and take the opportunity to enjoy journeys that can be made without taking everything but the kitchen sink with you!

The mum-to-be magazines are full of checklists on the subject of how to get ready for nature's great human earthquake. One in front of me now includes being sure to pack:

- A sponge to wet your partner's lips – which will also give you a great excuse to look the other way when you need to.
- A large hand-held mirror – so she can have a peep at what's going on down there.
- Something for you to chew on – Mars bar, or whatever. It could be a long time between meals and you'll need some energy.

- At the very least, pack a disposable camera.

Other things not to miss are:

- Checking the route to the hospital. Even doing a dummy run if need be. And being sure you know where the after-hours entrance is.
- Having money or a phonecard for the hospital phones – as mobile phones can't be used in a hospital.
- Keeping the car topped up with petrol or having the number of a cab firm within easy reach.

Everything Will Change

A Matter of Time

It will never be too early to begin rewriting your priorities and replanning your schedules. The countdown is on and soon you won't be able to do it all. It may be rugby, the lads, church or voluntary commitments, overtime at work or whatever. But something *will* have to go.

Don't fall for the lie that they don't need you until they're old enough to kick a football around the park with you, or build sandcastles on the beach. The truth is the wise dad is the one who invests time in their son or daughter from the word go.

And, of course, it's not just the time they demand, it's also the time they absorb. Forget doing anything quickly from now on! Packing and then checking that you have the full complement of baby kit – spare nappies, baby bottle, dummy,

playpen, car seat, highchair, steriliser unit, wipes, sick bag, cuddly toy, most treasured piece of old blanket, et al – takes time.

Given the chance to put the clock back I would have held a directors' meeting with Rosemary to work out how we would budget our time and responsibilities in the same way we budget our finances. The agenda would have read something like –

1. Responsibilities – who will now do what?
2. Time:
   a. Assessment of new demands
   b. Action plan to fit it all in
3. Money – how will we afford it all?

33

A Matter of Stamina

Of course it's not just your time that's under pressure. Your new arrival is also going to test your stamina. Coming your way – ready or not – is a little something with:

- The ability to cry at a sound level of 117 decibels – just less than a pneumatic drill.
- A likelihood of crying two hours a day for the first three months.
- Boundless energy – eventually able to run, race, wrestle, swing, slide and more for twenty-five hours a day, eight days a week.
- An enquiring mind that can ask the question 'why' with mind-numbing regularity and monotony.

 Top Tip: *Assume nothing will be the same again. Because it won't be!*

A Matter of Judgment

Should you be blessed with more than one child, that's when the fun really starts. You'll soon discover that every child's deep-seated sense of justice will make you just as much a referee as a parent.

If you doubt what's ahead let me tell you a story. Two children – with eyes bigger than their bellies – dribbled over the same piece of chocolate cake. Not for the first time, their father saw the beginnings of what, experience told him, could quickly escalate into World War Three. He thought about the best approach and then explained that they could have half each. One was to cut the cake in half. The other was to choose first. A smiling father then had the pleasure of watching an exhibition of precision engineering that was a sight to behold!

Juggling Your Work and Home Life

You are about to enter a phase of life that's somewhat like a juggling act. The common factor between your work life and your family life is you. Get that right and most of the rest will fall into place. So how do you do it? Here are a few ideas.

You need a clear sense of what really matters. There's a story told of an American President who summoned a young senator to a very important and privileged meeting along with a group of his peers. 'Sorry, Mr President,' came the reply, 'My son plays his first game for his school softball team that day.'

'I understand perfectly,' responded the President. 'We will have to move the meeting.'

I would like to believe the story to be true. Because, when it comes to making choices and defining priorities, what you regard as most significant is ultimately going to define your decisions.

You need to take decisive action. Juggling becomes increasingly difficult with every new ball an assistant throws to the performer. Of course, the assistant has no concern. It's not their job to juggle. Just to watch and 'so what' about the implications. Your new arena is going to be like that. Those who have been throwing you balls will keep on doing so. They may do so with a look of pity or regret but the balls will keep on coming.

There's only one person who can shout 'stop' and it's you. Struggling on in the hope that it will be all right on the night is not going to solve anything. Take charge. Make decisions. And do so sooner rather than later.

> **Top Tip:** Be clear about where your priorities lie and take the decisive action needed to achieve them.

You need an outside perspective. You may think you are making it all hang together. But what about those around you – especially your partner? Their input will help you evaluate and create a balance.

There have been moments when Rosemary has rightfully exploded because I have been so focused on survival that I have totally failed to see what my juggling act has been doing to her and others. So much better is an occasional 'summit' in which the person who knows you best can have their say.

You need to put your family in your diary. 'Tea with Tommy' may not sound impressive in your daytime scheduler when placed next to 'Lunch with the MD' but it is the wisest approach. Otherwise you'll quickly find your vital family commitments are things you fit in around the 'big things of life'.

As someone who is more creative than organised, I know this to my cost. Which is why I start each year by filling in the dates of all my children's birthdays in my diary – plus wedding anniversary, Valentine's Day, Mothering Sunday and so on. But don't stop there. Schedule unbreakable – and I mean unbreakable – diary commitments for 'family business' just for the sake of it too.

You need to steer clear of multitasking. There I was, a baby on one knee, a toddler telling me about their day, the TV on as I half-watched the evening news. One ear was open for the telephone call that could come at any minute, and my mind was on tomorrow's planning meeting. I was everybody's and nobody's.

The simplest way to balance home and work – though hardest to achieve – is to keep the two in their own boxes.

And to aim at doing one thing at a time with everything you've got.

> **Top Tip:** *Focus on doing one thing at a time with everything you've got.*

You need to take time for you. There was a moment when a consultant psychiatrist looked me in the eyes and said, 'You're not dying. It's just that you have been running too close to the edge for far too long.' He gave it some fancy name. Most people call it burn-out.

The squeeze had been on – between work and family – with me in the middle. I'd had time for every one but me, with all of us ending up paying the price.

At the heart of the problem was the fact that I'd spent all my energy – physical, emotional and spiritual – on others, without looking after myself. What seemed brave at the time seems foolhardy now. But hindsight can make any fool into a genius.

Just as your partner needs time to herself – on which there will be more later in this book – so do you. The priorities you set have to include time and space for fun, laughter, relaxation, exercise and recreation.

Add to that a balanced diet, not allowing decisions that need to be made to hang over you and avoiding keeping your emotions bottled up and you will be well on your way to being the person you need to be to make it all work.

It's the 'I'm OK' Kids Who Do Best

Making Your Child Feel Secure and Special

What's the chance of your kid underachieving, dropping out of school, creating a baby when they shouldn't, acting up, turning to drugs or running with the crowd? The answer to that conversation-stopping question is: 'It all depends.'

Or to put it more positively, what's the likelihood of them building secure relationships with their peers, fulfilling their potential, staying on the rails, confidently facing new challenges and coping effectively with the frustrations and difficulties of life? The answer, again: 'It all depends.'

So what does it depend on? On how they feel about themselves – positively or negatively. It's what the jargon-generators call 'self-esteem'. This is the most important quality a child can take with them into their teenage and young adult years – to feel good and confident about who they are. This one overwhelmingly crucial factor is the greatest key to their future.

The encouraging news is that your child's self-esteem is not dependent on whether they have their own bedroom, visit Disney, or own a mountain bike. But nor is it locked in their genes – with an outcome as predictable as their ability to sing in tune. The daunting news for every parent is that, for the most part, a child's view of themselves comes directly from you.

Self-esteem – or the lack of it – springs from a child's deeply ingrained experiences of how others, particularly their parents, relate to them. The words they hear and the attitudes they experience create your child's sense of their intrinsic value. The messages they pick up from you are bound to effect the way they see themselves – either positively or negatively. So how do you build up your child's sense of self-esteem?

Two recent reports defined those children with a high measure of self-esteem as 'can-do' kids and those without it as 'low can-do' kids. They revealed that 'low can-do' boys – those with little self-esteem – are:

- More than four times as likely to smoke;
- Five times as likely to use drugs;
- Twelve times as likely to often feel depressed; and
- Almost five times as likely to think of suicide.[4]

'Low can-do' kids are also far less likely to be socially active or interested in a world beyond themselves. For example, they are less likely to read a book or a newspaper, listen to the news or play sport.

The story as far as girls are concerned is not that much

different. In fact, research increasingly confirms that an important factor in determining an adult woman's sense of worth is the quality of the relationship she had with her father.

So what can you do as a dad that will build your child's self-esteem? Nearly all research points to one overwhelming answer. It's the time and attention you give them. It's as simple and profound as that.

41

Boys with low self-esteem say their parents:

- Are unloving;
- Aren't very helpful;
- Don't listen to my problems and opinions;
- Won't let me make my own decisions;
- Don't offer guidance;
- Fail to lay down the right rules;
- Don't treat everyone in the family equally;
- Try to control everything I do;
- Treat me like a baby;
- Take no notice of me;
- Argue with me often.

'Can-do' boys, for example, are:

- Over three times as likely to talk through their school-work with a parent; and
- Three times as likely to be hugged.

In contrast, 'low can-do' kids are likely to:

- Receive less parental guidance in terms of clear rules and open discussion;
- Participate in fewer shared meals and activities;
- Receive less encouragement to show their own initiative.

Although raising children is ideally a two-person responsibility, the studies show a father's role to be highly important. 'Can-do' girls are most likely to be those with a father who is supportive. And 'can-do' boys are:

- More than twice as likely to have a dad who spends time with them; and
- Eight times as likely to have a dad who talks through their relationships.

In contrast, and to put it starkly and simply, 'low can-do' boys tend to be those who have received a low level of fathering. So what can you, as a dad, do in this most vital area of your child's development?

Let Them Know You Love Them

Make sure your child knows you love them. It's never too soon to start or too late to continue. From the cradle onwards I wanted my kids to think they were the absolute 'bee's knees' so far as their dad was concerned. Today, I still want my hulking grown-up offspring to be equally sure I love them and respect them.

 Top Tip: *It's never too soon to start telling your child you love them.*

And don't be fooled into thinking this slushy stuff is just for girls. Those who know about these things tell us boys need this kind of affirmation as much, if not more, than girls.

Do It with Words

It's not British to say how you feel. You can tell how true this is from the conversation between a husband and wife where she said, 'Darling, you never tell me you love me any more.'

To which came the stoic reply, 'I said I loved you on our wedding day. If anything changes I'll let you know!'

The penny first dropped for Rosemary when she watched an American friend sweep up her two-year-old in her arms, and smother him with kisses while saying, 'Ian, I love you, I love you, I love you.' It was utterly not what British people do. But for Rosemary – and eventually for me – it made a huge impression.

The child *knew*. It was not a matter of him guessing, assuming or hoping. He *knew*. And he would walk taller and more confidently as a result. British or not, we followed suit.

When it comes to building self-esteem, there is no substitute for simply saying as often as you can, 'I love you', 'You're great', 'I'm so proud of you'. And the best time to do it is when your words are not a reward for anything specific they have done.

 Top Tip: *Don't keep your affection to use as a reward – spring it on your child as an unexpected surprise!*

There are ways to do it with words that are not spoken and these can carry even more weight. OK, so it's not cool or British. But so what? Try a note slipped into a lunch box or into a packed bag when they are going away, or a few well-chosen lines on a birthday or Christmas card.

Don't leave it until they are in their teens. Otherwise the only response will be, 'Give it a rest, Dad! Leave it out!' The older they get the less public they will wish you to be. But do it.

Do It with Actions
Those who know tell us that physical touch makes all of us feel better mentally and emotionally. Children are no exception.

Some families are more 'touchy-touchy' than others – which is a shame as touch speaks volumes. For example,

45

there is nothing like a long hug to say what you want to say. Make it a habit when they are young and keep going.

And don't underestimate the impact of:

- A back scratch
- A neck and shoulder massage
- A foot massage
- Holding hands and linking arms
- A kiss on the cheek
- A pat on the back
- A ruffle of the hair
- A nudge in the ribs.

There are also loads of non-verbal ways to say 'You're OK' and 'I love you' that don't involve touch. A wink, a smile, or sometimes just being there.

Other actions that can express thoughtfulness and love include a little surprise present or an unexpected outing. It's not the cost that matters but the thought and care involved. In fact, never imagine the size of a gift is an effective way to demonstrate the measure of your love. Kids know when they are being bought.

The Ten Things Every Child Longs to Hear

1. I love you.
2. You did that so well.
3. I'm so proud of you.
4. You did your very best.
5. Well done.
6. You are a great kid.
7. I trust you.
8. You said that so clearly.
9. You make my day.
10. I just love to have you around.

Do It by Treating Them as Special

We have a family ritual that each child, to mark their birthday, is taken out for a meal of their choice all by themselves. We make sure it is somewhere other than a fast-food place, to give time for talking and relating in a setting where they can get our undivided attention. On those all too rare occasions when I have travelled alone with one or more of my kids I have always tried to find an excuse to eat together on the way.

Perhaps the biggest thing we have done as a family is plant a tree to mark the birth of each of our children. When we move we'll take cuttings and start again.

It's amazing the symbolism these trees have come to convey. On the night of the 'great storm' that swept the south of England in 1987, Rosemary was out in the driving rain binding together the split trunk of Aran's tree. (I slept through – being as impervious to storms as I am to crying babies after nightfall.) Aran – it had to be his tree! – knew what the act of sacrifice represented.

Of course, there are less dramatic ways to convey the 'I love you and you are great' message. You can:

- *Take them out on their own* – cinema, sports, or whatever.
- *Decorate their room* – with them having a meaningful role in deciding what it will be like.
- *Go shopping* – even this can do the trick, as long it is for them and not to top up the fridge!

Do It by Listening

One of the hardest things for a father to do is to really listen to their child. Why does this happen? Because us men don't cope well with small talk. And that's the problem when it comes to really listening to our kids. The talk doesn't come any smaller.

However, when someone knows they are being listened to

– as opposed to only hoping they are being heard – it makes a fantastic difference to the way they see themselves.

Keys to being a good listener are:

- *Taking the initiative:* 'Let's go and grab a burger together.'
- *Asking open questions:* 'How are you getting on with your new teacher?' 'How are your friends doing?'
- *Shutting out distractions.* Put down the newspaper. Turn off the TV, the car radio, your mobile phone.
- *Not lecturing.* If conversations always end up with them having to listen to you they will soon learn to keep things to themselves.
- *Looking them in the eyes* and giving them physical and verbal signals that show they are getting through. Nods, grunts and 'I see' will do for starters.
- *Reflecting back to them what you have heard.* 'That must have been a great game to have had such fun.' 'So Mrs Brown said the hamster will have babies.' 'That means you have some more school work to do.'

 Top Tip: *If you really want to listen to your child, minimise your distractions.*

If you listen then you'll know their:

- Favourite room in the house
- Most enjoyed outing
- Best friend

- Favourite colour
- Greatest worry
- Happiest moment
- Most treasured possession
- Favourite TV programme
- Dream for the future.

If you have younger children, something to try at bedtime is the 'Sad and Glad Game'. They tell you one thing during the day that made them a little sad. And one thing that made them glad. Try it. You'll learn a lot. And so will they if you play too.

And remember, once they reach their teenage years – far from slacking off, it's time to redouble your efforts. In those traumatic days of self-doubt, self-consciousness and raging hormones called adolescence, they'll need you more than ever – even though they won't often show it. Each new minor zit – which takes on the significance of a major earthquake – delivers one more reason for teens to feel bad about themselves. An atmosphere of listening and loving acceptance is your top priority.

Do It by Being There

Jim Carrey's character in the classic comedy film *Liar, Liar* is a dad who never keeps appointments with his son. In revenge, the boy is granted a wish binding his excuse-ridden father to telling the truth for a whole week. Your kid has no such chance to strike back at you – but has the same emotions when it comes to you being there for special events. And remember, what may not seem special to you may be of vital importance to him.

My own response to 'being there' has included eleven consecutive seasons of Saturday mornings watching my sons play football. That's one consequence of having four sons. What astounds me was how few other dads ever made the effort. This had a positive double-impact on my boys. Other dads couldn't bother but theirs could.

I also went to watch my daughter when she started ballet classes at about the age of three. It was such a wildly hysterical sight I all but bit through my hand to stop myself laughing out loud. Such is the price . . . !

Opportunities for you to 'be there' are endless – and don't be misled by a child saying, 'It's all right. It doesn't matter.' Deep down to them it does. Get to everything you can – concerts, sports activities, open evenings, car boot sales, fundraising events, nativity plays, and the rest.

It also matters what you wear! Part of the impact of being there is not to turn up in anything that would embarrass them. If necessary get them to inspect your intended outfit. And listen.

Use the Power of Praise and Encouragement

Praise and encouragement are two vital tools in any parent's 'toolkit'. But they do very different things. Praise tells your child that they've done well when a task has been achieved. Encouragement, however, is what motivates a child to go for it or complete a task in the first place. It builds their self-esteem, keeps them going and also motivates them to try again next time.

Here are a few phrases to write on the back of your hand for the right moment:

- 'I like the way you're working out that problem.'
- 'Knowing how good you are at this, I know you're going to make it.'
- 'I have faith in you and your decision.'
- 'Look how far you've come. That's great.'

 Top Tip: Praise, not criticism, is the most effective way to encourage good behaviour.

Incidentally, praise does more than build your child's self-esteem. It is also one of the greatest provokers of good behaviour. Nine out of ten children say being praised helps them behave better. Why? Partly because it leaves them feeling good about themselves. But mostly because praise gives them the attention any normal person desires and they don't have to find some other less sociable way to get it.

Two warnings, though:

- Don't let your attitude convey an impression that something is only worth doing if you are guaranteed to succeed. Show them from your words and attitude that it's more important to do, than to do well. In this way you'll give them permission to practise, improve or even fail.

- Don't hold off giving praise because of a fear that they will become complacent. Praise is one of the greatest motivators for them to do it again, only better.

Don't Use Praise with Conditions

Praise is not praise when it's delivered like a barbed-wire sandwich. So avoid handing out praise with one hand and taking it away with the other by using phrases like, 'You did that brilliantly – shame you can't do it like that more often.' Or 'That was a great job. And about time too.'

Try to remember praise is not a device to manipulate your child into performing to your expectations and standards. It is about:

- Helping them feel good and comfortable about themselves.
- Helping them know they are accepted and valued for who they are – not what you want them to be.
- Recognising the effort they put in and the progress they make.

How to Build Your Child's Self-Esteem:

★ Show and tell them you love them for who and what they are – not for what they do. And do it over and over again.

★ Respect their feelings with the same kind of respect you look for from others.

★ Emphasise their good points rather than their bad ones.

★ Avoid comparing them negatively with others.

★ Listen – really listen – when they are talking and let them know you are.

★ Don't miss an opportunity to praise them for what they do.

★ Encourage them to express their talents and abilities – and minimise negative feedback when they do.

★ Be consistent in the rules you establish – and fair and reasonable in the way you enforce them.

★ Be available – so they know that they are at the top of your priorities.

By using the right kind of encouragement you'll give your child a growing belief in themselves and their ability to solve problems and complete tasks. You'll also help them to develop the courage to accept mistakes and failure as part of life – and to learn from them.

Be Their Coach

It was while on a birthday outing to an ice rink that my eyes were opened. We'd arrived early, birthday boy and friends in tow. As a result, the first twenty minutes were spent watching an aspiring junior Olympian learning his craft under the eyes of his coach. Time and time again he attempted the perfect triple-whatever, only to crash to the ice. What struck me was the repeated and patient reaction of the coach – a constant flow of *'Well done'*, *'Almost'*, *'Perhaps next time'*.

I can't verify the figure but I was once told athletic coaches know they need to give seventeen positive comments for every negative one. True or not, it's a principal we dads would do well to heed.

Be Patient and Let Them Do It

Self-confidence and self-esteem grow in the soil of being trusted – even trusted to make mistakes.

> **Top Tip:** *Don't undermine your child's confidence by finishing a task yourself.*

Feed Them Positives

Consider the less-than-subtle difference between 'Don't forget to brush your teeth' and 'I know you'll remember to brush your teeth'. Or between 'Make very sure you are careful with that – you know how clumsy you can be' and 'I know I can trust you to take good care of it'.

A childhood during which they constantly hear 'Be careful', 'Mind out', 'Don't forget' is one where they will end up feeling less able and confident than should be the case. Ultimately the outcome is probably going to be the same in terms of the state of their teeth, or your family heirloom, but the impact on the way your child sees themselves is going to be vastly different.

Don't Compare Them Negatively with Others

Words can be deadly, none more so than the ones that you use to compare your child unfavourably with someone else – especially if the someone is their own brother or sister. Words like: 'Look at David's tidy room – why can't yours be like that?' And 'If only you would put in the same effort as Clare just think how much better you'd be doing.'

What your child actually hears in situations like this is more like, 'Someone else out there is doing much better than you are. I love them more than you – you're a failure.' You may view your comments as motivational. But to them they are as poisonous as arsenic.

 Top Tip: Don't ever fall into the trap of comparing your child with others.

Don't Have Mixed Motives

As you spur your child on to success, do a motivation check on yourself. Is all this for them or for you? Are you sure?

Be careful not to confuse your ambition *for* them with fulfilling your ambition *through* them. Think about it. Is all this positive fathering, encouraging and coaching you are doing about enriching their life or yours? Is it about how *you* will look in the eyes of others or because you have their best interests in mind?

Getting clear on that vital question alone will make a powerful difference to the way your child responds and the way their self-esteem flourishes – or not.

Show Them Respect

Respect involves treating them as valuable human beings from day one. Actually that's not hard on day one! It's a little further down the road that the battle begins. Respect is not only about your attitudes, it's also about your *actions*.

Set Reasonable and Reachable Standards
Your child came from the factory with an in-built ability to perform random unreasonable acts. This should come as no surprise because so did you. Therefore keep your expectations of them reasonable. Base them on what a child can realistically be expected to attain at each stage of their development.

Spilled drinks and wet pants come with the territory for four-year-olds, no matter how careful they try to be. On their journey to becoming as perfect as you are things will get messed, muddled and missed. What seems careless or thoughtless to an adult is often the very best a child may be able to do. At times they will be blind to the consequences of their actions – because they have yet to learn enough to know any better. Be sure your expectations of them allow for this – and so give them the respect they deserve.

I'M SORRY TO SAY THIS SON, BUT YOU'RE FAR TOO PERFECT TO ALLOW ME TO MAKE THE MISTAKES THAT WILL HELP ME GROW AS A FATHER.

Expect the jobs they do to take twice the normal time and create three times the normal mess. Assume damage will be done. Plan for each child to do something serious to the family car at least once before they leave home. That's how life is.

Such an attitude is not a cop-out on the issue of bad behaviour. Just a plea for realism. Without it resentment will slowly replace self-esteem.

Be Willing to Say 'Sorry'

'Sorry is the hardest word' goes the song. And it's even harder when it's your child that deserves to hear it from you. The easiest thing in the world is to save your face by exerting your authority.

If your child is really valued it won't be so hard to say 'Sorry, I got that wrong', 'I'm sorry I was bad-tempered', 'I'm sorry I didn't listen', 'I'm sorry, if I had the chance to do that again I'd do it differently', 'I'm sorry I hurt your feelings'. And to your child – whatever their age at the time – it will speak volumes.

Ask for Their Help and Advice

Nothing boosts a child like being valued and respected by being asked for their 'wisdom'. 'How do you think we should tackle this?' 'Any ideas about . . . ?' Phrases like this tell your child so much.

Encourage their school to treat them as a whole person

Despite the vital role that a child's level of self-esteem plays in their future success, it is not a subject found on the school curriculum. Nor are teachers trained to set it as a goal for a child's long-term development – not that this is the fault of the teaching profession, who are generally driven by the academic expectation of employers, the government and even parents themselves. As a result, some aspects of the education system can work against what really matters for your child. If so, in their interests, stand your ground.

Above all, make sure that those teaching your child understand what you value most from their education. Good friends of mine who have twin daughters told me of an encounter with their girls' Year Head at a parents' open evening. It began as they sat in silence listening to the educational shortfalls of their daughters. The list went on and on, finally coming to a halt when the teacher asked if they had any questions.

They thought for a while and then asked, 'How well do our daughters repond to direction and discipline from the staff? Are they respectful?'

'Yes,' came the puzzled reply.

'Do they contribute willingly and helpfully in class

discussions and relate well to their peers?'

'Well, yes they do,' came an equally puzzled answer.

'And are they developing good social skills and growing in self-confidence?'

'Well, yes.'

'Have you ever told them any of this?'

'Well, no.'

'Then would you please do so by including it on their report – because we regard this just as vital in their development as is their academic progress.'

Foundations that Stand the Test of Time

You may ask yourself, will it all be worth it as I work to build my child's self-esteem? Believe me, it will. At the times when your relationship with your child is under stress, you will be glad your love has been shown in such tangible ways. Because then you'll have a bedrock foundation to keep the building upright through life's storms.

One of my sons went through a time of trying our patience to the absolute limit. I'll spare you the gory details. Trust me. Finally there came a time when something had to change. Life was becoming ever more difficult and unbearable at home.

Behind me was the knowledge of a foundation of constant affirmation and assurances, in word and action, that he was loved no matter what. In that context I found myself saying, 'Son, you know I love you. In fact, if it came to it, I would even die for you. But right now I really don't like you at all.'

I had been able to tell him the truth about himself – something it was vital for him to hear – in the context of the certainty that my claim to love him had unassailable substance. It made all the difference.

You and Yours

Dads and Their Kids

Know Yourself

Dads differ. It may sound obvious to you but it's a big issue. Unless you get to grips with your distinct contribution to this relationship, both you and your child could end up missing out on some of the riches involved. Let's start with an aspect of who you are that you may never have thought about in terms of being a dad.

Know Your Temperament

Your temperament has nothing to do with being 'temperamental'. It's about the fact that you have a preferred – or natural – way of behaving. Some of us head for the inside lane of a motorway as soon as our exit sign is the merest blip on the horizon. And we run the rest of our life in much the same way. Others hang on and keep their options open until the very last minute. And do much the same with everything else in life. Our temperament – our preferred way of doing things – impacts every aspect of our behaviour.

Have you ever applied for a job and been given a question-naire to complete in which some questions seem to have nothing to do with work? They're testing your temperament! They want to know how your basic approach to life relates to the job in mind.

The experts call this 'psychometrics', but it's not only

relevant in the workplace. It has a huge part to play in the relationship between you and your child. Your temperament will impact the way you function as a dad just as much as the way you do your job.

My temperament means that I tend to see negatives rather than positives. Ask me how my holiday went and I'll say, 'It was great except that ...' I walk into rooms and fight the urge to put the pictures straight. If ever I get to see the Sistine Chapel I'll no doubt point out what is wrong with the ceiling.

This is bad news for my kids because it's the way I tend to function with them as well. As a result I have often got it wrong. When it comes to school report time, for instance, I ought to be locked up. The overwhelming good becomes masked by a minuscule amount of bad.

It's not that I'm mean-spirited but, rather, that this tends to be the way I am programmed. And I ignore the consequences at the peril and pain of my family.

If you ever get the chance, read a good book on the subject of temperament – you'll learn a lot about yourself. Meanwhile, here's the very briefest of outlines setting out the four basic ways in which temperament – our most natural way of behaving – shapes the way we respond to those around us.

1. *Our focus of attention.* Some people get their energy from relationships – the world outside them. They are talkers, relaters, crowd-lovers. In contrast, others get their energy from within themselves. They are readers, thinkers, more private people.
2. *Our method of acquiring information.* Some people learn exclusively through the use of their senses. They 'know'

65

because they have seen, heard, measured, tested and so on. These are practical and factual types – good at remembering and working with facts. In contrast, others rely on information that transcends hard facts. They look at the 'big picture'. Almost without knowing where ideas come from they can identify fresh approaches and new ideas – intuitively.

3. *Our way of making decisions*. For some, this is all about engaging their brains, weighing up the issues, and looking for logical conclusions. They are the analysts who will tell you what's wrong and what's right. In contrast, are those whose conclusions are based on values – what matters and who matters. They are people of tact, who care about whether something is agreeable or disagreeable.

4. *Our way of relating to the world*. Some are naturally planners and organisers. The world in which they live is to be regulated, controlled and managed. They are out to create structure and order because that's the way they are most comfortable to live. On the other hand are those committed to flexibility and spontaneity. They relate to the outside world by gathering information and setting out to understand what they find and control it. They are adaptable rather than rigid.

So how should all this 'pseudo-techno' science impact you as a dad?

None of these alternatives are either right or wrong – they are just different. Nor is it likely that you will be at one extreme or the other on any of them. Taken together, however, they show how distinctly different each of us is from the next guy – and also from our child. I tend to get my energy by being around people, to have a natural flow of creative ideas, to value truth at the expense of how people may feel about it, and to want to keep all my options open until one second to midnight. You may be exactly the opposite. Neither of us is 'right' or 'wrong' – we are simply different. But the impact on the way we raise our children will be highly significant.

And, of course, your child is unique too – and their right to be so will impact your relationship with them and should also shape your expectations of them.

 Top Tip: Give yourself permission to be 'you' and your child to be 'them'.

The lessons to learn from all this are simple but profound.

- *You have the right to be a dad 'your way'*. Some of those wonderful dads out there who so easily intimidate you were made differently to you, but not better than you. I'm in awe of Steve who has built a garden play-house for his kids that seems to have everything but running water and a Jacuzzi! But I'm not him – and he's not me.

- *You need to work on those aspects of your life that are not your preferences*. If you are naturally shy, for example, don't allow that to end up restricting the social contacts of your children. If you are a bit of a 'boffin', don't be closed to the charms of rap, dance or 'garage' music, the joys of football in the park and the spontaneous and creative aspects to life your child deserves and needs to experience.

- *You need to value your own qualities.* The blend that makes up who you are represents a distinct contribution to the relationship you will build with your child. The components represent what you are best at. Make the most of them.

Top Tip: *Work hard at understanding yourself – it will help you to understand your child.*

Know Your Strengths and Weaknesses

Then there's the question of character – all those 'qualities' that best express who we are. Do any of the following ring a bell?

- Loyalty
- Rashness
- Dependability
- Trustworthiness
- Impetuousness
- Generosity
- Impatience
- Over anxiousness
- Calmness
- Meanness

- Pride
- Ambition
- Assertiveness
- Competitiveness

Which of these – and other – aspects of character are most likely to impact the quality and effectiveness of your fathering?

Let's face it, every time your child gets on a sports field, steps onto a stage or takes an exam, your own feelings of self-worth are likely to be out there with them. The two very powerful emotions of pride and embarrassment are there too. Be sure they don't dominate in a way that distorts your sense of reality and undermines your relationship with your child.

Know Your Child

What Makes Them Special?

Kids differ too. Just like their dads. Give any two children the same parents, the same environment and identical treatment and – without doubt – they will turn out differently.

As it happens, all ours have much the same ability to be brash and loud in public. But for all their brashness, our five are still very different from each other despite coming from the same set of genes and being reared in the same environment. The contrast between the first two says it all.

Kristen as a toddler was a thug. When he arrived in the playschool crèche, mothers swooped to lift their own little darlings out of the danger area. He was the one who karate-

SETTLE AN ARGUMENT, DAD — WHICH OF US IS MORE UNIQUE?

kicked a neighbour's new glass front door – in homage to Superman – shattering it into a million very expensive pieces.

Yet Joel, who followed in his footsteps, was the opposite. 'Wet' was far too dry a word for him. On holiday in Spain, at a resort close to the airport, we could confidently let him toddle off down the beach. Because every few minutes or so another plane would pass overhead – sending him dashing back to us for safety.

 Top Tip: *Treat each child as an individual in their own right and not a clone from home.*

Some kids laugh at clowns and others scream blue murder. Some take to animals and others want them taken away. Some head hotfoot for the white-knuckle rides and others blanch at the Noddy train. And it's all OK.

Some children are more comfortable with their own company and their own inner world of reading and doing. They are more naturally quiet and reflective. Others prefer to get their charge of energy from others – endlessly seeking company and companionship. They are more likely to be outgoing and enthusiastic. It's OK – both are normal and deserve to be treated as such – rather than being forced or cajoled to become like the other.

Some children have a tendency to be logical and deductive – steering towards maths and sciences. Others are naturally intuitive with the ability to be quick with words and new ideas. Again, both deserve the respect of being treated well for who they are. Your job is to allow them to develop their strengths, not squash their personalities in any misguided attempt to create bland 'household' uniformity.

There are also just a few children who came from the factory with an innate ability to be tidy. They are a rare and endangered species who'll never fit that definition of a teenager as 'someone old enough to dress themselves if only they could find their clothes'.

Most are far more comfortable with a more relaxed approach to tidiness. Work out if what you see as the resultant 'mess' is due to them being lazy or genuinely part of their temperament – recognise them for who they are while also doing your best to help them live in harmony with others. It's no good being angry with them for who they are – it's not their fault. Whether it's nature or nurture – in the end it's down to you, not them!

So what is it that makes each child so different and unique?

Know Their Temperament

Gradually as your child grows and develops, their preferred ways of gathering knowledge, drawing energy, learning and planning will become clear. The outcome is going to have a profound impact on –

- The way you relate to them; and
- The way they learn.

This makes it important to –

Understand Their Unique Qualities

Where does your child draw their energy from – the world outside themselves or their world within? It's all too easy to assume it must be the same place you get your buzz – and so find yourself on an entirely different wavelength to them. Don't try to make them into someone they are not – by attempting to drive a more thoughtful and reflective child into having a greater outward focus. Or forcing a born activist to read, read, read.

The same is true in the area of values. For every child who sees no problem in telling it just like it is, there's another who would prefer to say anything rather than hurt someone else's feelings. For them, any kind of confrontation is next to impossible. Again, as a dad, this involves you in affirming your child's rights to be who they are, while at the same time helping them to cope with the world as it is. This principle holds firm for every area of your child's temperament – including their ability (or not!) to manage their time, plan their homework, relate to friends and so on.

A child's temperament can have a huge impact on their sense of security. Imagine for a moment your child is most comfortable in a world of order. They prefer things tied down and defined. And imagine you are different – always wanting to keep your options open 'just in case'. Think of the impact this difference is going to have on them.

For example, in this instance, think how much better it would be for them if the family holiday was not one where you launched into each day wondering what might turn up. To have a basic game plan on the table, even if it ended up being changed, would make it all so much more enjoyable for them. As would an 'Our Meals for the Week' list stuck on the door of the fridge at the start of each week.

 Top Tip: Discover which learning style suits your child best and use it to their advantage.

Understand the Way They Learn

Your child's temperament will also impact the way learning works best for them. As a dad you will want to take that on board because they will best respond to one of four main learning styles. Your child could be –

- *An imaginative learner* – these are curious and question-ing children who learn through listening and sharing ideas. They tend to see the big overview more easily than the detail.
- *An analytic learner*. They expect the teacher to be the main way they receive information as they sit and assess the value of what is presented. They learn best from the way most teachers have traditionally been taught to teach. As a result they tend to be the kind of children on whom teachers focus at the expense of others.
- *A commonsense learner*. These are the hands-on children – who use their own ideas to work on problems and to solve them. They like to know the theory before putting it into practice.
- *A dynamic learner*. These are children who follow hunches and sense new directions and possibilities. They are looking for new ideas, solutions and ways to do things.

You may be surprised at how soon in a child's development these distinctives can come to the surface. I remember taking one of my sons for his two-year assessment by the community child care worker or whatever. One test involved a handful of hundreds and thousands – the minute confectionery that gets sprinkled on the top of cakes. She spread it on the table with the instruction for him to pick some up and hand it to her.

Her expectation was the strands would come one at a time, so giving her an understanding of his eye and hand co-ordination. But the kid had a different approach to life.

Instead he licked his finger, dabbed it into the pile and offered her the result. It was fast, effective and very bright. What surprised me was her reaction. Not admiration or respect for his creativity, but muted annoyance. He had not done it *her* way.

Such situations will be repeated through the life of many of our children. Their style is different and they may miss out unless they are recognised for who and what they are.

Understand Their Character
The qualities you like or dislike about yourself lie latent in your child. Some will blossom – for good or ill – all by themselves. It's here your guiding hand – and shining example – matters. A key is to recognise the positives and build on them. For example, if a hint of generosity or kindness blossoms, feed it the fertiliser of encouragement and reward for all you are worth.

Understand Their Nature
There is another telling aspect of your child that can vary, as you will discover sooner rather than later. Some kids are naturally compliant. They go with the flow. They ask 'How high?' when you say 'Jump'. And do *what* they are asked *when* they are asked without an outbreak of 'I hate you' Kevin-itis.

And then there are the other sort – those wonderful non-compliant kids who test your patience to the limit. To them, life is about pushing the boundaries at what seems to you like every turn. Pull their string and the words that come forth are 'Why should I?' – possibly followed quickly by 'Won't'.

What did you do wrong to get one of the latter? Probably absolutely nothing. It is all just part of life's rich pattern. Some kids are like that and some are not. You just have to treat them for who they are and know that being a dad to a compliant kid is a whole lot easier than being a dad to one who isn't. However, if you're a dad to a non-compliant kid, be comforted with one important thought. In the long run, who is going to make the most waves in life?

There you are in a restaurant – with your non-compliant kids insisting on making mini-ski runs out of the salt – and adding peas to make trees. At the next table is a nicely ironed and pressed family – with children who seem not to even know the word 'boo', never mind think of saying it to a goose. Don't feel intimidated. Think of all the pent-up creativity in your brood just waiting to burst forth. And all the unrelenting boredom in theirs. Think potential.

A friend of mine had to listen to her daughter's supposed shortcomings from her junior school teacher. To which she replied, 'You obviously can't spot leadership qualities.'

See Things through Their Eyes

If you have seen the film *Honey, I Shrunk the Kids* you will know what it is for someone to experience a familiar world from a totally different perspective. Alongside the terror of confronting life-sized ants was the encounter with a world of wonder and adventure. Your child has just such a world waiting for you to explore.

It's a world of make-believe, imagination, creativity and fun. It's a world that can only be seen though their eyes and from their perspective. To most dads it's another planet. To your child it's home. Many adults are far too sophisticated to pay a visit. They will admire from a distance but never act like natives or learn the language. Their emphasis is on turning the child into a little adult just as fast as they can – rather than exploring the adventure of childhood themselves.

It's fine doing those mechanical and sporty things with them. But also be sure to explore the world of imagination and make-believe as well.

Your Responsibilities

Every human being – and your child, believe it or not, is one – has four dimensions to their life. They are physical, social, spiritual and intellectual. Each aspect of who they are needs your attention. These four dimensions are like the four legs of a table. If one leg is short and underdeveloped the whole table will be unsteady.

 Top Tip: Keep your eye on every aspect of their life – social, physical, spiritual and intellectual.

Physical Fathering

This is the stuff of doing. Your part is to take care of your child's physical needs. That means making sure they have a room to untidy, clothes to mess up and food to drop on the carpet.

Physical fathering also includes keeping your kids physically fit, making sure they eat the right things, and helping them feel secure. For a child to stay happy and healthy you need to be sure these physical elements are in their life. In practical terms, this will involve things like:

- *Exercise*. Get them out there doing anything you can.
- *Cooking meals with them*. This could be a treat for mum – and not just on Mother's Day. But make sure you also clean up afterwards!
- *Doing house jobs*. Involve them in your cleaning and mending projects. Giving them at least one specific role – ideally this should be one simple task they can be responsible for each week. Make sure they deliver and praise them for what they do.
- *Getting involved with any sports team of which they are a part*. Manage, train, provide transport for, or just bring the half-time oranges. Your child would love you to be there teaching them skills and the qualities of sportsmanship.
- *Keeping track of their TV viewing and use of the Internet*. If it is over-obsessive you will discover 'Why don't you read a book for a change?' carries very little impact. And you'll also find a phrase which goes, 'Let's go out together and . . .' gives you a much better chance of success.

- *Sharing a common hobby with your child.* There are tons of hobbies for you and your child to enjoy together. Everything from collecting to modelling to puzzling. And make it their choice rather than yours.
- *Budgeting with your child.* Show your child how to make their pocket money last; how much to set aside for entertainment, clothes, toys, saving and the like. And when it goes wrong, don't bail them out more than once.
- *Taking them shopping.* Encourage them to take care of the money or at least to count the change and be on the lookout for the best bargains. Don't wait until they are a student for reality to drive them in that direction. Show them now how to save money by buying no-name brands,

using coupons, spotting discounts and special offers. If you are extra brave, you could include the incentive of letting them keep half of what they save you.

- *Giving them their own plot of land to cultivate*. Or at least a pot on the doorstep or a hanging basket or a few cacti. Make it theirs to be responsible for – with a little help from you.
- *Getting a pet*. This is a case for some realism. My choice is goldfish over a Great Dane anytime. And hamsters have an unfortunate habit of greeting your return by laying on their back in a very rigid position and holding their breath for several years. But whatever you go for involve your child in the work involved.

Social Fathering

Your child needs to learn how to live in a world beyond their own. And to understand it's not enough for anyone just to do their own work well. Each of us exist as part of a community – family, friends, school and so on. More than that, some of our best efforts in life should go to benefit others beside ourselves.

You have a job to do here. It involves helping your child to make friends and relate effectively to others. Perhaps some of the following ideas will work for you as you help your child develop their ability to function on a social level.

- *Get to know your children's friends*. The interest you take in your child's friends will demonstrate that friends matter.

Know their names and what interests them.

- *Make your home the place to be.* Try to cultivate a 'drop in' atmosphere – where other kids want to visit. An ever-open tin of chocolate biscuits is one effective source of attraction!

- *Throw a party for their friends.* There are subtle ways to chaperon a party without intruding. Cook a barbecue, for example.

- *Involve them in adult conversation.* Their confidence in relating to others will grow as the result of them being listened to and involved. A simple way is for you to give them room to answer the questions asked of them rather than butting in to do it for them, or forever tidying up their answers.

- *Teach them social skills.* Give them opportunities to see you being polite, showing respect and conducting conversation. And encourage them to put what they see into practice – particularly when meeting strangers, answering the telephone and so on.

Spiritual Fathering

We may no longer be a religious society but we are still very much a spiritual one. Your child is growing up in a world where seven out of ten adults 'sometimes' or 'often' think about 'the meaning of life'.[5]

Most adults have come to the conclusion that there is more to life than can be experienced through their five senses alone. Many believe they want more out of life than money, sex and

81

power. And each child surely deserves opportunities to consider the options as soon as they can grasp their significance.

Of course, no dad should be happy to see their child go headlong and unthinkingly into a personal conclusion about life and its meaning. At the same time, leaving a child to 'make up their own mind' at some point in the future with an almost total lack of information to go on is to sell them short. A wise dad steers a careful course between the two extremes. Here are some ways that would help:

- *Share your own convictions if you have them*. Help them to catch the sense of wonder that you experience and let them in on what it means to you.
- *Help them encounter the great faith stories of history*. For instance, there are some wonderful children's Bible storybooks available from any good bookshop and some excellent video cartoon series featuring them as well. Add to that the C S Lewis creations like *The Lion, the Witch and the Wardrobe* and similar stories and you are on your way. After all, why should Pokémon get all the action?
- *Pray for your children*. From the moment each of our children were born, whoever put them down at night said a simple prayer over the cot. As a result they always had a sense there was a dimension beyond themselves.
- *Help them become concerned about issues of justice and tolerance*. One way to bring this alive is for your family to sponsor a child in the Third World through a reputable relief and development agency.
- *Use the religious seasons*. Christmas, Easter and so on provide a helpful time to explore their meaning. Your

child's school may well be doing the same and you could develop this further through a project or reading.

- *Take them to a place of worship.* Many couples use the birth of a child as an opportunity to explore their own view of life and do so by finding a welcoming church to attend. This eventually provides an environment in which their child can make discoveries of their own.
- *Give them opportunities to encounter beauty.* Even if you live somewhere where sparrows cough rather than sing, find ways for your child to take in the wonder of nature and creation. The Discovery Channel is not enough to give them an encounter with magnificent landscapes, beautiful flowers, wonderful animals – all of which can communicate a sense of wonder.

 Top Tip: Give your children lots of opportunities to see beautiful sights and things.

Intellectual Fathering

This is your 'developing their mind' role. And it's not just about pushing them to do well at school. Educating our kids is a way of life, whether it's in the car, in the park, at the shops, around a meal table or at the work bench. In settings like these we can share the skills of life and convey the values that matter to us.

Intellectual fathering involves stretching their mind and

DO YOU THINK WE'RE GIVING OUR KIDS ENOUGH INTELLECTUAL PARENTING?

I DON'T UNDERSTAND THE QUESTION.

experience by encouraging them to think and discover. It's here the world of TV can work for and not against you. Let's be realistic, your kid will watch TV whenever and wherever. That's how life is. Occasionally one comes pre-programmed with a burning desire to study the violin or to establish a vast collection of moss and fungi. But even they are likely to have a ravenous appetite for anything that comes hurling their way down a cathode ray tube.

So cash in by making the content of what they are watching your starting point. The opportunities are endless:

* 'Why – do you think he felt like that?'
* 'Where – is this place they are travelling to?'
* 'What – would you feel like if that happened to you?'

- 'How – do you think they are feeling now?'
- 'What – would you do if that was you?'

You can also:

- *Help them with their homework*. The challenge here is to be their coach, not their producer of answers. To help them learn, not to get them through.
- *See yourself as their primary teacher*. In fact, this is exactly what you are. They learned to talk from you. They learned to walk from you. Now just keep going.
- *Encourage them to do their best*. Measure success in terms of how hard they tried, not how well they did compared with others.
- *Read to them*. Of all the temptations you face as a dad there is none bigger than the one to turn over six pages at a time when reading to a preschooler. Resist this and you can resist anything.
- *Talk about current news issues*. Never put them down with a 'Didn't you know that?' Instead provoke their interest with questions like, 'Can you find the place on the map?' And 'What caused that, do you think?'

Get that lot half right and you will be doing a great job.

Keeping the 'Glow' with Your Partner

Dads and Mums

And then there are three. An intruder has arrived to disturb the calm and order of the relationship you had with your partner. It may be your first or your umpteenth new arrival. But believe me, it's going to make a difference. Now there's even less time and energy for everything – including each other. Now there's a competitor for your love and attention.

If this is your first, the early months can be a real shock to the system. Nothing's ever going to be the same again. This reality can dim the light of even the best relationship. So how can you keep the glow? And what if this isn't the first? Or it's some while since the tiny feet stopped pattering? How do you face the same issue?

Be Realistic

The birth of your child – and the months that follow – will
have a significant impact on your partner. It's not just stitches
and stretch marks, there's also the impact on her emotionally
and physically.

Her Mind

Worry is a big issue for a new mum. 'Is that really supposed
to happen?' 'Is it OK that I feel like this?' One way to face
the pressure of new parenthood is to reassure your partner
that:

- It's quite normal for the birth of a child to leave a woman
  feeling exhausted. It's natural for her not to feel like doing
  anything – including coping with visitors.

- Babies are commonly born with slight health problems. And though they may cause much anxiety to the parents, they rarely constitute any lasting danger to the child.
- It's not compulsory for a mother to 'fall in love' with her infant at first sight. Despite what you may have seen at the movies, many don't.

 Top Tip: *It's quite normal for a new mum to feel exhausted and emotional for some days or weeks after the birth.*

Just coming to terms with these three areas will help to establish a sense of reality for a mum and a less anxious time for you.

Her Emotions

I can't remember exactly what I said – but my words had the impact of reducing Rosemary to a heap of trembling and sobbing jelly. What I do know is these were not cruel or abusive words. In fact, under normal circumstances they would have had little impact at all.

But these were not normal circumstances. It was now four days after the birth of one of our children. And that was the crucial difference.

The birth of any of your children introduces significant changes in the new mum's make-up. As a result, she's as likely as not to experience 'the baby blues' – a brief spell of mild

89

depression, leaving her feeling emotional, exhausted and tearful.

It's all down to what's going on with her hormones, normally combined with a lack of rest or interrupted sleep. The signs are easy enough to spot. You may find her:

- Crying for no apparent reason
- Being excessively impatient and irritable
- Being over restless and anxious.

These difficult and seemingly irrational moments come to more than half of all mothers. The good news is they usually disappear on their own – often as quickly as they came. Most often all that's needed is a little time for your partner's body to heal and for her to be allowed lots of extra rest. Which is where you come in – big time.

If this doesn't help, and things seem to go downhill each day, it would be wise to get your doctor involved. A brief period with the right medication can work wonders.

Although in most cases the baby blues go on their way quickly and easily, it's not always the case. Your partner may be among the one in ten who go on to suffer postnatal depression.

Postnatal depression usually rears its ugly head within weeks of the birth. But it can surface weeks or even months later. Despite the delights of the new baby – and the love and care of others – the mother's tiredness, irritation and loss of concentration are compounded by the guilt she feels over not coping. This can result, for her, in feelings of:

- Sluggishness and exhaustion
- Sadness and hopelessness
- Lack of appetite
- Problems with sleeping
- Memory loss, poor concentration and confusion
- Excessive worry over the baby
- Uncontrollable crying and irritability
- A lack of interest in the baby
- Deep-seated feelings of guilt, inadequacy and worth-lessness
- A fear of harming the baby or herself
- Exaggerated mood swings from high to low
- A lack of interest in sex.

She will have good days – when the sun seems to shine again. And bad – where the symptoms leave her feeling ashamed, guilty and isolated.

Some women may feel anxious rather than depressed. This is characterised by intense moments of:

- Panic, fear and a sense of doom
- Rapid breathing and a pounding heart rate
- Chest pains and hot or cold flushes
- Shaking and dizziness.

It's here that four cheers for the medical profession are due – because this is where the answer lies. Despite any protest from your partner that 'It will be all right and I don't want to cause anyone any trouble', talk to your doctor as soon as possible. And make sure your partner takes advice and the medicine offered.

For you these will be difficult days. I know, I've been there. The worst part is feeling whatever you do is wrong or not appreciated. The other is your feeling that she is no longer the same person that you fell in love with. Hang in there – it's part of life and it will pass. Meanwhile:

- *Don't try to reason with her.* Emotions and logic don't mix. However irrational her feelings or fears may be, arguing won't make it different.
- *Try to be patient.* Stick it out, knowing it won't always be like this.
- *Let her express her feelings.* And treat them with sympathy. Don't force her into doing anything she doesn't feel ready for.
- *Don't ignore your own needs and feelings.* Ask for help too if you need it.
- *Do all you can to get her to take rest* – and to keep on doing so.
- *Get her to eat regularly* – even if she does not feel hungry.
- *Don't add to her stress* – by making major decisions like moving house or changing jobs.
- *Don't be too hard on yourself* – it's natural to feel frustrated so reward yourself when you have achieved something, however small.
- *Encourage her* – with the reminder that every woman who suffers from postnatal illness comes through it – things *will* change.

Her Body

One thing is guaranteed. A new mother will be tired. Caring for an infant is hard work with no option of flexitime or time off in lieu. This means you now have a relationship with someone who may not for some time to come be as energetic and full of life as you once knew her.

The drain physically and emotionally for a mum can seem endless, right through every stage of childhood. It's not just the workload – which can never be underestimated – it's also the overwhelming level of responsibility. 'Are they developing the way they should?' 'Does that cough signal anything out of the ordinary?' 'Is it all right to let them . . . ?'

Share the Load

Traditionally, it has been the mums whom society has tended to regard as its 'frontline' parents – the ones with day-to-day responsibility for children. Dad, on the other hand, is just a playmate – adding to the fun, helping out now and again when it's convenient and, at the other end of the spectrum, being the ultimate weapon in times of crisis.

Seeing and Doing

You need a very different mindset to this. One where you understand that you cannot act as a spectator while the work piles up. For men, this is not that easy to achieve. We seem to have a different way of seeing things – for instance, our definition of the word 'tidy'!

93

To make things worse, I've discovered that women tend to be more observant than men and far more intelligent. They not only have radar vision equipping them to spot household chores that are sitting up and begging to be attended to. They also know exactly what needs to be done to see the job completed.

In a man's world the solution is simple. We expect the one who sees and knows to point out the need to the one who is as blind as a bat and as useful as last month's TV guide. But this is not a man's world. In reality, many women find it hard to express their needs by saying, 'Please would you . . .' They can also resent having to do so to someone who, 'if you love me', should surely know anyway.

In other words, there are two worlds colliding here – your world of 'logic' and their world of 'feelings'. This may not make much sense to you but – if you genuinely want to maintain the glow – you need to learn to play by her 'rules', not yours.

Try to set time aside with your partner to talk about the day-to-day tasks that, if left undone, could turn into sources of tension. And then – take the initiative! Try to come up with solutions that – although they may mean extra work for you – suit both you *and* your partner. It may include you:

- Making a superhuman effort to see what to a normal male eye is invisible – and acting accordingly.
- Coming up with a defined list of responsibilities, which you diligently attend to.
- Creating some kind of wall chart or day planner that allocates specific tasks to you.

Top Tip: *To help share the load, talk to your partner about what needs to be done as well as your role in making it happen!*

Their Expectations

Your partner has expectations of you in your fathering role just as you do of yourself. But don't assume they are identical. My expectations of what was involved in being a dad were based on the role I had watched my father play – which was not a big one! However, Rosemary had other role models to look to – and had watched the film *Three Men and a Baby* far too often in my view. As a result, her expectations and assumptions were very different to mine.

These differences between your expectations and hers can relate not only to issues like who does what. But attitudes to money – spend or save; discipline – forgive or burn at the stake; bedtime – right after tea or following two yawns, and so on.

Many a couple have had a 'wobble' because they were running on two different sets of assumptions. The only way to keep the 'glow' in your relationship is to talk these issues out. Don't be afraid to seize the initiative with a question like, 'What are your expectations of me now I'm a dad?'

A big part of this process is simply to make clear to your partner your commitment to work hard at being a dad and to be specific about the responsibilities you recognise are yours. Many dads shy away from actually making the commitment of saying what they intend to do as a way of steering clear of getting into trouble for not doing it.

And to add insult to injury, when they do – from time to time – step into the fathering arena, they see it as being 'far beyond the call of duty' and so wait for the applause. After all, when you've committed yourself to nothing, anything looks great.

Be Practical

Take a firm grip on your expectations now the nipper has arrived. The glow will begin to go if you try to carry on as though nothing has changed.

Because of her depleted energy levels and increased workload your partner needs more of your time and fewer of your demands. There's a need to adjust your lifestyle where possible. For instance:

- Try to adjust your working hours so you are around for at least one of the most pressurised parts of your partner's day.
- If you are in a job that can involve work outside of normal hours, avoid taking work home if you can.

The sexual side of your relationship is also likely to change – particularly in the short term. 'How do you know when a man is thinking about sex?' goes the question. 'Whenever you see him breathing' goes the answer. You may be the one in a million who is different. But I doubt it.

Unless your partner is a very remarkable woman, her libido

is going to wane somewhat as she gives her emotional and physical reserves to more pressing issues.

 Top Tip: *Be ready for your partner's sex-drive to dip as she gives her energy to more pressing issues.*

You need to:

- Be romantic – without any ulterior motive. And remember, if you are planning a cuddly evening in, the smell of sick is not conducive to anything. Air freshener works wonders.
- Be patient – because your turn will come.
- Be prepared for touch that doesn't always signal the end result as full scale rumpy-pumpy.

As time goes by, teach your children always to knock on your bedroom door before they enter – night or day. And rehearse the excuse you will use the first time they forget!

Talk and Listen

At the heart of every glowing relationship is open and honest communication between the two parties. It's a situation where both of you truly believe your words, needs and feelings are heard and understood by the other.

Communication of this quality demands:

- Uninterrupted and undistracted time.
- Listening to what's being said rather than just the words involved.
- Reflecting back what's been said so the other knows they have been heard.
- Speaking as much about feelings as facts.

Such communication doesn't just happen – which is why it is so rare. So work hard to carve out the kind of time needed and then take the initiative to make the right kind of conversation happen.

Make Time for Each Other

There is no substitute for an evening without your child – or better, a whole weekend. You may have to fight off your own and your partner's guilt. But remember, a generation or two ago, such an idea was automatic and so easy to achieve.

Until only about fifty years ago the majority of mums had relatives living close by. People like their own mum, grandmother, sisters, aunts and so on. It was the most natural thing in the world to drop off little Harold or Doris in order to find space and respite. No one ever seems to take this aspect of social life into account when reflecting on the lower levels of divorce and emotional illness at that time.

Today you may live in Grimsby and have all your potentially supportive relatives scattered to the four corners from Cornwall to Canberra. So you need to act smart to compensate. Here are some simple ideas.

Trade with Another Couple

Somewhere out there is another couple just like you – who equally need some time and space. If your partner has joined a parent and toddler club you have a starting place to look. The idea is simple. You leave your child with the other couple for a weekend and escape. And you do the same for them in return.

 Top Tip: *Find a way to take time out by yourselves by trading time with another couple.*

Learn to Grab Odd Moments

Keeping the glow involves finding time to talk, listen, relax and just be together. Busy parents know there are few large slots of time in today's family where that can happen. So you have to squeeze them in – which takes some planning and discipline.

Each couple will have their own particular lifestyle but here are a few hints.

- Spend at least one evening a week with the TV off.
- Take up an interest you can do together.
- Use an answerphone to shield messages – and respond to

personal calls when your partner is not around. Or simply unplug the phone.

- Send cards, write notes, e-mail each other. Let her know that you are thinking of her – it will work wonders.

Deal with the Green-Eyed Monster

Once you were the centre of attention. Yes, you. The apple of her eye. Now, particularly if you're a first time dad, someone else shares that treasured pinnacle – and at times you feel as though you are about to be pushed off.

It's not unreasonable to have feelings of resentment and jealousy in a situation like this. But it's not good. No matter how hard you try to cover up, the green ooze of jealousy will eventually seep through the cracks. At some point, probably in the heat of disagreement, the truth will dawn.

So make sure you are in touch with your inner feelings. Ask yourself if you are being realistic or a bit of a nerd. Perhaps, in reality, you *are* being neglected. Don't be afraid to express your struggles on this one with your partner. But be sensitive and don't demand – that never got anyone anywhere.

Be Committed

We live in days of built-in obsolescence. When did you last take an electric toaster to be mended, for example? The obsolescence factor has also hit relationships. The statistics tell us marriages are being dissolved faster than ever before. And 'committed' relationships outside of marriage are dissolving still faster.

It's in this context your partner knows she is not the woman she was. Children have that impact. It's hard to keep the sparkle, the trim figure and the shiny hair when there are so many plates to spin and nature is causing too much flesh to head south. It doesn't take much to imagine her fears. Even if they are not that you have eyes for 'some young, slim, sexy, energetic thing' down the street, they are that you love her less than you once did.

Whether or not you actually ever said, 'For better for worse, for richer for poorer, in sickness and in health', she needs to know that's the basis of your relationship now. The security of that commitment is the ultimate power boost to keep the glow in your relationship.

Top Tip: *Make sure your partner knows yours is a 'for better or worse' commitment.*

That's why marriages last longer than 'committed relationships'. Knowing that both parties have a 'we are in this together no matter what' attitude creates a freedom to be vulnerable, open, transparent and honest that is far less likely where one doesn't exist.

To be practical:

- If you have them, dust off the wedding photographs and put them in a more prominent place.
- Watch your wedding video.
- Write a letter or send an e-mail to your partner that expresses your commitment.
- If you've never moved from having a committed relationship to one of marriage, give it serious thought.

Be Romantic

To be honest, if you need to be told how to be romantic then you are in trouble. And if you've reached the stage where bringing her flowers is met with, 'So what are you saying "sorry" for now?', you need more help than this chapter can offer. Hopefully it's not that bad. Which means my contribution is to remind you to do what you know how to do as often as you can.

That means:

- Don't stop doing the lovey-dovey things you did before the invasion of the tiny feet.
- Remember anniversaries, Valentine's Day and special events with extra commitment. They are of far more significance than we mere men could ever appreciate.
- Spring a surprise from time to time – it's the thought not the cost that counts.
- Tell her you love her – in words spoken and written – time and time again.

That's my recipe. Now go bake the cake.

When It's Extra Tough

Stepdads, Distant Dads and Single Dads

The shape of families has changed dramatically over the past generation or so. We have moved from the 'nuclear' family to the 'unclear' family. There's little value in discussing why all this has happened. It's simply a reality. And it impacts tens of thousands of men – for whom their challenging role as a dad is extra tough.

For example:

- Steve is a stepdad confronting all the complex issues and tensions this involves.
- Dave faces the reality of visiting rights and does his best as a distant dad following his marriage break-up.
- Mike is a single dad since the death of Carol.

All three – and thousands just like them – have mountains to climb and sometimes the road is pretty rocky.

Stepdads

Steve, a stepdad, is part of one of the most challenged and fastest growing segments of society. If you are a Steve you're part of one of the half a million stepfamilies in the UK. Over 2.5 million children are involved in stepfamily life.[6] And if there was ever a tough fathering assignment this is it. You have stepped into an emotional minefield.

At one and the same time you may be having to cope with:

- Dealing with your own past – and the wounds that may so easily be involved.
- Establishing a relationship with your new partner in what may be less than ideal circumstances.
- Settling into this new family situation with your partner's children and possibly your own as well.

If that sounds anything like you, congratulations. You deserve high praise for being willing to take on what, by any account, is a challenging task. But if 'willingness' alone was enough to guide you through the minefield ahead, life would be easy. The truth is, it's a lot more complicated than that. So how can you defuse some of the traps lurking beneath your feet?

Understand Your Role

Recognise the facts. In reality, you are not the father of your partner's children. That means she is their 'prime' parent. Of course, that doesn't let you off any hooks. It just changes the hooks you are on.

> **Top Tip:** Make sure you allow your partner to play the role of the 'prime' parent.

Your partner is, at least in the early stages, their prime parent. Your role? To be more like a mentor than a father. Standing alongside your partner, you give the children an added perspective of wisdom and support. And can become a vital source of strength as they grow and mature.

Despite the importance of your role, it's your partner who carries the ultimate responsibility for raising her children – though you may come to earn an equal share of that responsibility over time. What you do possess, however, is the potential to influence these children and win their respect. So remember:

You are not a replacement dad. It's a mistake to picture yourself as coming off the bench as a substitute in extra-time – to replace a failed striker and save the day. Try to take on the role of their father and you may well antagonise them rather than winning their trust.

Instead, work to create your own distinct and healthy relationship with your stepchildren. Get them to accept you as the person who is now loving and caring for their mother. Not as a replacement for their dad.

Top Tip: *Get them to accept you as a person, not as their replacement dad.*

Don't force her children to call you 'Dad'. When your new partner chose you, her children probably had little say in the matter. You were their mum's choice, not theirs.

This factor alone makes it wise for you not to further force your partner's decision onto her children – by making them call you 'Dad'. To try it the other way is the fast road to resentment, especially with older kids. Instead, let them set their own comfort zones as they relate to you. If your goal is to be called, or thought of as, 'Dad', patience is the best route forward. In time it may be rewarded – providing you work hard to win their love and respect.

Face the Fact of Their Father

Like it or not, there *is* a father in the wings – hero or villain, it matters not. You are now playing a leading role on the centre stage – but there are some pretty influential noises off. How best can you cope with them?

Face the reality of the father's existence. It's tempting to try to make this a new day by pretending the past didn't exist. 'Let's put it all behind us and start again', is the temptation. 'There's no need to stir up memories and bring back all the tears.' But that denies the reality of the situation.

No matter how hard you try to leave the past behind,

you will have to deal with the invisible presence of an 'ex'
– who at times you can almost hear shouting through the
keyhole.

 Top Tip: *Don't try to pretend their father no
longer exists or try to look good at his expense.*

You can't forget him, and neither can the children. If you try
to keep his bones in the closet, sooner or later they will come
leaping out. Most probably during a confrontation with your
children.

Instead:

- Be open and honest about his existence in all you say and
  do.
- Let the dad know you are not after his place.
- If at all possible, encourage him to be involved with his
  children – remembering he *is* their father.
- If there's a need, do what you can to bring about recon-
  ciliation between him and his offspring.
- Never try to make yourself look good at his expense.
- Don't try to close down any discussion about him.
- Do everything you can to avoid the kids being caught in
  the crossfire between the two of you.
- Don't set out to prove you can do it better. This is not a
  competition.
- Speak positively about him in the presence of your kids.

Go Easy on the Issue of Discipline

Perhaps the most explosive issue for a new stepfather is the discipline of the children involved. Do you do what their dad would do? Do you leave it all to their mother, no matter how much you disagree? Do you let them get away with murder for the sake of a quiet life?

Allow their mother to be the final custodian of discipline. She has a biological right on her side against which there is no argument. So let her be the final arbiter of the rules of the house so far as her children are concerned. And, when issues arise, make sure any role you play is seen as supporting her and at her request and expectation.

This means the two of you need to agree on what rules the home will run to. That may well involve compromise on your part. Especially if your view is considerably different to the one she and the children's father worked to. And remember, the introduction of some new heavy-duty discipline from you is not going to make you the most popular man on the hill.

Don't let them see you as the enemy. It is oh so tempting to come into a new relationship with an iron hand, determined to make things right from now on. But be aware of the damage this could cause to your relationship with her children.

You can appear to be the enemy in ways you may not have considered. Like insisting on rearranging their food intake and table manners, taking charge of the TV remote control and setting new standards for bedtime.

New brooms may be OK in a work environment – where it doesn't matter if you are not liked and you can go home at

the end of the day. But they are unlikely to 'sweep as clean' at home.

Be flexible. The major problem is you are not on a level playing field. It's tough enough for a regular dad to set and maintain rules in the home. But you have some big disadvantages. You have no authority based on a biological link – so there's no automatic reason why your stepkids should take any more notice of you than anyone else. More than that, you can all too easily be seen as an intruder wanting to do things your way.

This means 'over my dead body' statements or too much direct confrontation where there can only be one winner are not going to serve you well. Before you launch into territory like this you have to have already won your stepchildren's respect. When they have come to love and trust you, you'll

111

be on safer ground to make your mark.

Be flexible too over things like their mannerisms and personal habits. Remember, they may not like your 'funny little ways' very much either! Instead, take the initiative and show them unconditional acceptance. Being willing for them to be who and what they are will encourage them to accept you more easily.

 Top Tip: *Be open and willing to accept your partner's children for who and what they are.*

Expect to be tested. Every stepchild is going to test the rules and every stepchild has double the reason for trying. It is often a way for them to express their pain at what has gone on in the past. Their anger for what they think you have done by coming into the home. Or an attempt to put the strength of your love and commitment to the test to see if it's real.

Even so, don't be afraid to say 'no'. But do steer clear of getting out of your pram or jumping to conclusions. Above all, try not to take rebellion too personally. Remember there's probably a lot more going on under the surface than you realise.

Have Realistic Expectations

You and your partner have dreams of creating a new and wonderful happy family. But your stepkids may well lack a commitment to any such perspective right now. Like a new pair of shoes, this new family is going to take some getting used to. So in the early days expect some blisters, discomfort and the odd uncontrollable squeak before everything settles in.

The children you have inherited are also likely to be very different from you – with their own distinct temperaments, interests, views on life and characteristics. Whatever you do, resist the temptation to try to make them like you.

So instead of regarding them as 'disappointments', accept there's no real basis for your stepkids to fit into any of your preconceived notions. Work at being a healthy model of someone who cheerfully adapts to your new family members as they are – faults and all.

Talk Straight

There is a lot you can communicate without using words. But sometimes they are essential. In this respect there are some things well worth saying face to face when a stepkid is old enough to take it in.

For example, it will help to:

- Tell them you know you are not their dad. And you accept, in their eyes, you may never be so. Yet this will not stop you loving them and doing your best for them.
- Own up to feeling inadequate. And that you want to hear from them when you get it wrong.
- Make it clear you have no intention of insulting them by trying to buy their love and affection. And that means

113

you won't try to outdo their dad when it comes to gifts, treats or pocket money.

- Explain that even if they can't stand you, because they love their mother you should try together to make it work for her sake.

Take It Slowly

Don't expect too much from your stepkids too soon. Instead, use this simple recipe for progress:

- Spend as much time with them as you can.
- Be patient, forgiving, kind and polite.
- Listen with an open mind.
- Affirm them for who they are.
- Don't generate confrontation.
- Give them respect and expect it back.

It's in this kind of setting that people develop trust and affection – and solid relationships grow.

Keep It Together as a Couple

Everything that's true for a 'regular' couple regarding strengthening their relationship and keeping its 'glow' is even more true for you and your partner. On top of everything else you have the stress of an unhappy past and a difficult transition to cope with.

The depth and quality of your relationship is important not only to you both but also to your stepchildren. They have seen one relationship end – and possibly even put some of the blame on their own shoulders. Now they need and deserve the security of knowing your relationship is in good shape.

 Top Tip: *Take time to talk about and plan how you are going to work together as a parenting team.*

So far as the two of you are concerned, there are two major reasons why you need quality time together. First, you need space and opportunity to nurture your relationship. Second, you need to think about and plan how you're going to work together as a parenting team. Your partner is a vital link between her children and you – because she knows you, knows them and is the one most informed about their father. Time invested in talking out the issues and planning your united response is going to really pay off.

Distant Dads

It's not a song you are likely to have heard but it is a favourite of mine – by a somewhat obscure country singer. He's sitting in a pick-up truck in eyeshot of the home where he once lived, painfully reflecting on what was and what isn't.

There's the fence he built, the wall he painted, the window behind which his young daughter 'laid her pretty head', and

115

the man who has now taken his place.

Dave doesn't own a pick-up truck but he has experienced the same feelings as the driver since the break-up of his marriage. As a distant dad, he knows only too well that there is a lot of pain and not much gain.

Your first thought as a distant dad may well be, 'I want to see my kids, I'm missing them' – on the basis that you feel incomplete without them. Yet they are in much greater need than you.

 Top Tip: *Remember that greater than your need to see your kids is their need to see you.*

Whatever may have gone wrong, if you are a distant dad like Dave – because the kids now live with their mum and you don't – you have a huge responsibility.

Boys are at particular risk. Our society is now feeling the 'ouch' of an adult male generation brought up with absent fathers. The result is a multitude of boys who have not known enough loving discipline and who lack sufficient social experience. As a result, they no longer feel the pressure to behave as responsible adults in society – to themselves and to others.

For girls it's a different issue – but equally crucial. Time and again, research has identified a direct link between the quality of a girl's relationship with her dad and her likelihood to have a casual attitude to sex in her teenage years.

Although these are the two big issues there are many more

– not least our old friend self-esteem. Dads have a huge role to play here, no matter where they may lay their head at night or park their pick-up truck by day.

In other words, you have a job to do – for their sakes. And it *can* be done. The 'can-do' kids study we looked at in the 'It's the "I'm OK" Kids Who Do Best' chapter also suggests it's not whether the father is in the home or not that matters so much as the quality of his fathering.

> **Top Tip:** *It's not where you live that makes the ultimate difference but the quality of your fathering.*

No matter how wronged or hurt you may be feeling, you can be an 'absent' dad and still do a great job. And be a 'present' dad and yet still mess up. Yet the tragic statistic is that three out of four divorced fathers lose contact with their kids in five years.

So, as someone has said, 'Whatever happens to your marriage, don't divorce your kids.' Let's look at some ways to make that a reality despite the difficulties you face.

Deal with Who You Are

Those lone fathers who really *want* to be fathers often feel a deep sense of pain, resentment and injustice because of what has happened. Usually it's because children are almost always put in the custody (or 'residency') of their mother.

117

There may be other personal issues too. Like the feelings of betrayal and failure. Or the guilt for having done the betraying.

This kind of baggage has to be left at the door of your continued role as a dad. The kids don't need to hear it or to be caught up in the attitudes that spring from it. What

DAD SAYS HE HASN'T SEEN ENOUGH OF US SINCE THE DIVORCE...

WELL IT'S UP TO YOU IF YOU WANT TO SHOW HIM YOUR "SKINNY DIPPING" PHOTOS FROM IBIZA...

happened has happened. They didn't ask for it, but they have to live with it. But now you must help them move on – not tie them to the past.

It is therefore in the best interests of all of you for you to deal with the issue yourself or get someone to help you – a trusted friend or a professional counsellor perhaps. You'll know when you have finally made it through the pain barrier. It's the moment when you are secure enough in who you are to be ready to lose face without striking back. When you can allow stinging words to roll over you without needing to retaliate, because what you now most want is simply to do what's best for your kids.

Keep Involved

- *Be creative.* Even if the access you are allowed to your child is limited, you can still be a part of their life. Letters, phone calls and e-mail all offer ways to keep in touch. Somewhere out there I'm sure there's a distant dad who has created his own Internet site for his kids to visit whenever they want. If you care, be creative.
- *Use time well.* When you are actually with your children make sure you genuinely engage them as human beings, rather than just turning up with 'the big gift'. Use this precious time to shower them with words and affection through meaningful conversation and genuine interest in their life and world.
- *Keep involved.* Involvement can also relate to other aspects of their lives beyond their home or new family. You can talk to their teachers, ask to see school reports, attend open evenings, go to concerts, talk to those who coach any team they play in.

How to Be a Helpful Distant Dad

★ Never use your children as a weapon in your fight to get even with your 'ex' or to justify yourself.

★ Never get them to tell tails or 'spy' on your 'ex' or the new man if there is one.

★ Never exploit their loyalty or ask them to choose between you and her.

★ Never make promises you can't keep.

★ Never use big presents to cover up for a lack of real fathering.

★ Never badmouth their mum – or the new man.

★ Never criticise the new house rules – even if it's not the way you would have done it.

Be Consistent

Don't underestimate the extent of the damage done to a child's self-esteem by the break-up of their parents. Almost always they hold themselves responsible in whole or in part. And, with their world now turned upside down, they've lost their essential sense of security.

You can help by providing a rock-solid 'presence' in their life through:

- Keeping your commitments to their mother.
- Remembering their birthdays and special events.
- Phoning to see how they got on at sports, school tests or whatever.
- Establishing a regular routine which you keep to – a

phone call on Thursday at 4 p.m, for example. Or a postcard that arrives every Tuesday.

> **Top Tip:** *It's better to give them your attention in a low-key, regular way than erratically through major treats.*

All children have a deep need to know and feel they are loved by their fathers. As a distant dad, remember a regular phone call once a week will say much more than several random visits to mega-theme parks scattered throughout the year. And no matter how big a one-off gesture you make, it will never disguise the decay of inconsistency.

Single Dads

One thing is for sure about being a single dad – it's not like the movies, where it almost always seems to be fun and a source of great laughter for the audience.

Statistically, most single dads have become so because their partner has died. Like Mike – a single dad since the death of his wife Carol. He suffered the loss of his life partner, his lover and the mother of his children in one cruel blow. That brings with it a huge pile of responsibilities to cope with – feeling lost, bereaved and alone, with little of the support and advice he needs.

Of course every situation is different. Some single dads

have great back-up from friends, wider family or their community. Some even have the financial means to support the dramatic change in circumstances. Yet there are common factors, no matter what the situation might be.

Get beyond 'Poor Me'

There is a significant choice to be made along the way for every single dad. It's to stop feeling sorry for himself and to start living again. To stop saying 'If only' and to start taking action to do what is best for his children.

 Top Tip: *If you are stuck in an emotional sludge pool, be sure to get the professional help you deserve.*

But that's never an easy journey. Emotions can have a will of their own and don't respond well to the command to 'pull yourself together'. Yet at the same time you have to move on – if only for the sake of your children.

If that's you – stuck in yesterday with no hope for tomorrow – then seek the professional help you deserve for the sake of your children if not for yourself.

See Your Children as a Positive Resource

I have lost count of the times people who have experienced tragedy have been helped on their way back to normality by launching a project. It's because of this that many caring charities have come into being – through the initiatives of those who have seen a loved one die or damaged. These initiatives are obviously valuable in themselves, but there is also an immense psychological benefit to those who started them.

My advice – make your children *your* project. Pour everything you have and are into them. They need it and so do you. In this way, what at first seems like an overwhelming loss and a new set of responsibilities actually becomes a means of restoring and building your own sense of self-worth in the process.

More than that, you have every reason to be confident you can do a great job. A major survey in the USA suggests that 'men make less neurotic "mothers" because they don't feel the same pressure to be perfect and are content to do the best they can'.[7]

Reshape Your Life

Recently I spent a couple of hours with a good friend on the first anniversary of his wife's death. He had been left alone to father sons aged seven and thirteen. This meant not only steering his sons through the emotional turmoil involved but also reordering his own life.

Helpfully my friend had been able to afford a reasonable level of paid domestic help. But he was wise to the danger. The easiest thing would have been to have her cook and serve the boys their meal each evening ahead of him returning from work. Instead he reshaped everything in order to cook and serve the meal himself – every evening!

 Top Tip: *Because you are the only parent they have, be sure to schedule the time that they need.*

He also knew that quality time with his boys was going to be more essential then ever because *his* time was the only parenting time they would be getting. Now firmly established in his diary, and on top of all the everyday times spent together, is a one-hour dedicated 'appointment' with each of them individually every week. Of course it's not as formal as it sounds but it always happens.

If you're a single dad you are going to have to take your own appropriate steps to make your kids the priority they need to be. I can't tell you what to do, but I do know it won't just happen left to its own devices. Only by you being proactive are you going to make this work.

Use Your Own Style

Although your kids will be missing their mum, the problem won't be solved by you pretending to be her. This is no Mrs Doubtfire exercise. They want you to be you and to get as much of you as they can get their hands on.

If your idea of adventure is something other than baking a cake, then leave the flour and eggs where they are. If it's splashing through puddles on a mountain bike getting more

I'VE TOLD YOU BEFORE: YOU'RE A GREAT SINGLE DAD — YOU DON'T ALSO HAVE TO BE A MUMMY.

messed up than their mother would have allowed, so what? As best you can, feel free to be you.

Just because their mum would never have left the house without making the beds or clearing the sink, it doesn't mean you have to live like that. And if you want to dismantle a lawnmower in the living-room, why not?

There's no reason why single dads should be expected to raise kids like mums do, any more than single mums should be expected to raise kids like their partners would have. Enjoy being a man and enjoy being a dad.

Working Smart

Your Average Dad's Survival Guide

Three university professors were discussing the complex issue of when life begins. 'Life begins,' said one, 'at the moment of fertilisation. That's when God instils a spark of life into the foetus.'

'No,' said the second, 'life begins at birth – because that's when the baby becomes an individual and capable of making its own decisions.'

'No, no, no,' said the third. 'You've both got it wrong. Life begins when the children finally move out of the house.'

I'd like you to believe there can be life for you as a dad long before that tear-jerking moment. And this chapter is my final offering to you to help make it so. To be honest, it's my glory hole. With all the things I want to say that won't fit anywhere else. Not that it's a dump bin. Rather, I hope, a treasure-trove.

Dig in, splash it all over and – I hope – enjoy. There are some ways to flourish as a dad – if you work smart.

Take a Long-Term View

It was Mark Twain who described his father as a very remarkable man because 'the older I get the smarter he becomes'. This is a phenomenon you will notice. At fourteen your child will regard you as a know-nothing cretin from the planet Nerd. Four years later they are amazed at how much wisdom and experience you have managed to cram into your cranium in such a short time.

So drink deeply at the well of patience and long-suffering. Tell yourself the 'terrible twos' will come to an end – even if only at the age of seventeen. Be confident that those whirlwind, 'where do they get all that energy from', early years will eventually slow down. Trust that the wretched, hormonally imbalanced, teenage, rollercoaster years simply cannot go on for ever – even though it may seem so at the time.

Hang in and do your best and it will be all right on the night. Or, at least when adulthood finally dawns. And when it does, you will be grateful for all you did to enhance the quality of your child's future and the sanity of your own life.

The Much-Quoted Toddlers' Rules of Possession

★ If I like it, it's mine.
★ If it's in my hand, it's mine.
★ If I can take it from you, it's mine.
★ If I had it a little while ago, it's mine.
★ If it's mine, it must *never* appear to be yours in any way.
★ If I'm doing or building something, all the pieces are mine.
★ If it looks just like mine, it is mine.
★ If I saw it first, it's mine.
★ If you are playing with something and you put it down, it automatically becomes mine.
★ If it's broken, it's yours.

Give Them Yourself

There is nothing more valuable you can give a kid than yourself. The temptation is to go for all kinds of substitutes. Special treats, PlayStation 2½, expensive holidays, a greater involvement from their mother and all the rest. But there is simply nothing like you. The time you give is irreplaceable.

Think about your own childhood. What do you remember most about your dad? The most likely answer relates to things you did together. For me it's not anything he bought me, or anywhere special we went. It's the times we played a scratch game of cricket in the park. And the afternoons, having caught seemingly any old bus, we sat on top in the front together and talked about what we saw.

 Top Tip: *Don't ever imagine there is any substitute for giving your kids your time and attention.*

For my kids, though we've done our best to make holidays memorable and splash out with presents at birthdays and Christmas, we have worked hard at the 'spending time' thing. As a result, they would tell you about the regular Sunday outings to feed the horses in fields near our outer-London home. Some great conker collecting forays. The family games of Monopoly, the Game of Life and Newmarket. The ritual of the big family meal on as many Sundays as we could manage and my notorious barbecues.

Remember, if it seems like a special event to take your kid for an ice cream, play a game of Fish, or to kick a ball in the park then there is something very wrong. Whatever you end up spending on your kids, there is nothing more valuable or worthwhile than spending your time.

Which leads me to a radical suggestion in our increasingly flexitime, shift-work age. Do your working hours force you to regularly miss both their breakfast and their evening meal? If so, is there anything you can do to be present at one of them, no matter what sacrifice is involved?

The reason for putting the clocks back and forward – daylight saving time – has a lot to do with not making children travel in darkness twice in a day. In the same way, can you move your schedule to avoid the darkness of missing out on your kids? It would be worth it.

The story is told of a father who came home from work late – again. Tired and irritated, he was confronted with his five-year-old son and the question, 'Daddy, how much money do you make an hour?'

'That's none of your business!' came the angry and frustrated reply.

'But, Daddy, I just want to know,' pleaded the boy.

'If you must know, I make £20 an hour,' he offered grumpily.

'Oh,' the little boy responded. 'And could I borrow £10, please?'

'No,' came the angry answer. 'First you ask how much money I earn and then you ask for some for yourself. Go to bed.'

When the man calmed down he began to think he might have been a little harsh. Maybe there was something the boy really needed. And he really didn't ask for money that often. Going to his little son's room, he said, 'I've been thinking, maybe I was a little unkind to you earlier. Here's that £10 you asked for.'

The little boy beamed. 'Oh, thank you, Daddy!' he yelled. Then, reaching under his pillow, he pulled out some more money. 'Daddy,' he said, 'I have £20 now. Can I buy an hour of your time?'

As someone has said, 'A child is an incredible being! Don't let yours grow up without you.'

Give Them Security

Kids today exist in a culture of fragile and disposable relationships. All around are friends who've seen their happy or not-so-happy home torn apart. The media, from the soaps upward, tell the same story: 'Don't expect any relationship, however good it might seem, to be permanent.'

Eventually there will come a point in your child's life, if you are a dad-in-the-home parent, when they begin to assume your relationship with their mother is at the same risk. That's why I guess I shouldn't have been surprised when, after overhearing me inappropriately raise my voice to Rosemary, one of my kids asked: 'Dad, are you and Mum going to get a divorce?' It was easy for them to come to that conclusion based on what they had seen and heard in the world around them during their few short years.

 Top Tip: *Make sure your kids know you are committed to them and their mother for ever – through thick and thin.*

Think of the insecurity this situation breeds for little, vulnerable minds. So what can you do? Take positive action:

Love their mother. One of the greatest things you can do for your kids is to love their mother and to make sure they know you do. With this in mind:

- Try as much as possible to keep your arguments out of their earshot – and your sulks and moods out of their sight.
- Display genuine affection for each other in front of them.
- Tell her you love her in front of them.
- Tell them you love her.
- Involve them in planning romantic surprises for her.
- Make a stonking great fuss of Mother's Day.

Let them know you are there for ever. Take opportunities to tell them you are committed to them and their mum 'no matter what'. Say it and show it.

That means:

- Never make threats about your commitment to your partner that reach their ears.
- When conversation turns to those of their friends whose parents have split up, promise them this will never happen to you.
- Take opportunities to assure them that, no matter what, you are going to stick together.

At the same time, don't underestimate how important the commitment of marriage is to kids. They don't know the statistics that 'permanent' and committed relationships are far more fragile than those of people who are married. But deep down they may have intuitively grasped the fact.

Kids deserve and need to be raised in the security of a 'better or worse' relationship. Because they know that when 'better' turns to 'worse' things are more likely to crumble if mum and dad are not married. Indeed, many a child sleeps more easily at night because of a belief their folks really are committed and determined to see it through. You owe it to your kids to do all you can to offer them every bit of security you can in every way you can.

If you are married, let your kid know you mean to stick to your promises no matter what. If you are not, think about what taking that step would mean to the security of your kids.

Show them unconditional love. Never let your kids think there is anything they can do to make you love them more than you do already. And nothing they can do to make you love them any less. In other words, leave them in no doubt that your love is unconditional. It is not given in exchange for their good behaviour or when they conform to your expectations and values.

 Top Tip: *Show them your love comes without strings – they can't earn it or lose it.*

Help them know the measure of your love has nothing to do with whether or not they are dry at night, learn their spellings, get As on their report, or conform to your views of sexual normality. They are loved forever by you no matter what they do or don't do, what they become or don't become.

That's not easy. But it's essential.

What are the keys to helping your child know they are

loved without any strings attached? It will help if you:

- Don't limit your expressions of love to when they have done something you approve of.
- Do tell them you love them when you are punishing them.
- Don't unintentionally link your expressions of love to reasons for showing it – 'I love you because you make me feel good.' 'I love you because you are the player in the team.' 'I love you because you do so well in school.'

Of course unconditional love has expectations – that it will be responded to with appropriate behaviour. Unconditional love does not say goodbye to discipline. It's not weak and wishy-washy. Many is the time I have had strong words and imposed considerable discipline on the basis of my unconditional love.

You are not expected to put up with simply anything your kid says or does. But what is called for is for your love to be unremitting, no matter what you have to put up with.

Establish family traditions. In our fast-moving and rapidly changing world, children need stability and security – and family traditions have a great role to play. They create a sense of what makes your family distinct and special from all the others in the world. They help define what it is your kids belong to that is true for nobody else.

In addition to the trees planted in our garden to mark the birth of each of our kids, our front doorstep is littered with a pile of large stones – because one always comes back from each of our family holidays, chosen by our children.

135

Top Tip: *Establish family traditions of your own to give your child a sense of security and belonging.*

There's a pond locally which, for years, we couldn't drive past without having to sing the silly song I made up in a moment of foolishness. And there's the 'let's pretend to be asleep game' we played when someone in the family came into the room. Not always, but enough to be fun. There's also the slightly odd version of the song 'Chick Chick Chick Chicken' my dad taught me, that I've taught my kids and that I hope they will teach theirs.

Traditions like this are part of what marks us out as 'our family'. They help provide the memories, continuity, identity and stability that help children feel secure.

Be an Example

For some reason our family routine had changed. For several mornings running I'd found myself in the bath the same time as one of my sons was cleaning his teeth. And at the end of his endeavour came a ritual that intrigued me. When all the deplaquing and spitting had been done he'd tap his toothbrush on the side of the hand basin three times. Why? I wondered. The next time I cleaned my teeth I knew. It was because I did exactly the same. He'd got it from me. I wonder if I got it from my dad and if he got it from . . .

As the toothbrush lesson shows, much of what we teach is communicated by accident rather than intention. And far more than we may realise. Driving down a narrow country lane and faced with a blind corner, I tooted the horn. In immediate response, from a child strapped into his car seat, came the outburst, 'Stupid woman!' I was quick to realise these words were those most heard in our car at the time the horn was usually put to use.

This means if I want my children to show respect, they need to see it in me. If I want them to be racially tolerant, they need to see it in me. If they want to see values of hard work, they need to see it in me.

Little Eyes upon You

There are little eyes upon you
and they're watching night and day.
There are little ears that quickly
take in every word you say.

There are little hands all eager
to do anything you do;
and a little boy who's dreaming
of the day he'll be like you.

You're the little fellow's idol
you're the wisest of the wise.
In his little mind about you
no suspicions ever rise.

He believes in you devoutly,
holds all you say and do;
he will say and do, in your way
when he's grown up just like you.

There's a wide-eyed little fellow
who believes you're always right;
and his eyes are always opened,
and he watches day and night.

You are setting an example
every day in all you do;
For the little boy who's waiting
to grow up to be like you.

Anon

The examples given me by my father have lasted all my lifetime. And so will yours, for good or ill. How you handle money, how you treat other people, how you establish priorities. In situations like this and more, what you model will make a significant impact on the way they grow up.

> **Top Tip:** Keep your eyes open for what you are teaching, even when you don't think they are learning.

While travelling through this territory, may I just add a word about dads and daughters? One day she will need to figure out what men are like and what she should expect from the one who becomes her life's partner. The first man she will ever watch is you. Hopefully you will prove to be a very significant example of positive manhood – consistent, trustworthy, sensitive to the feelings of others, making your family a high priority, keeping your promises, investing your energies in those around you.

With that kind of reference point, she'll have an invaluable measuring stick to spot the undesirable. And when some man lets her down she will know the male race are not all equally as flawed.

Discipline and Standards

Some of the least welcome words to be left on my mobile phone message system are, 'And I've told him you will deal with him when you get home.' That's because the issue of discipline is one of the hardest to get right.

Of course times have changed. Once it was easy. A couple of generations ago you took your belt to them, sent them to bed without any tea and that was that. No longer.

To me, for a dad to get discipline as right as it's possible to get it, you need to:

Set reasonable boundaries and expectations. If you have not started this book from the back, you will already have seen my thoughts on this in the 'It's the "I'm OK" Kids Who Do Best' chapter. To repeat myself, we need to judge our kids on the basis of what is normal and acceptable for someone of their age and not ours.

In addition, are your boundaries reasonable and fair? When it comes to issues like how far down the street can they go, what time are they to be in, and what they may wear, on what are your boundaries based? Is it your paranoia? What others may think of them and you? Or something much more reasonable?

 Top Tip: *Make sure the boundaries and standards you set are in their best interests rather than yours.*

Look round the bend. Don't wait for the event to hit you between the eyes. Decide what you would do should such and such happen or request be made. In this way you also protect yourself from that most cunning of all childhood strategies – the ambush. At the moment when you are having to do three things at once – and under pressure with all of them – will come the strike, 'Please, Dad, can I ...?' It's then you will be glad you have some words you had prepared earlier.

141

Be consistent. It sounds obvious but if rules and expectations shift according to how you feel at the time – or what's convenient at the moment – you are in for problems. It is easy to compromise because you are worn out at the end of the day or because you don't want to make a fuss in front of others. But fudge it this time and life will be even tougher the next.

Decide what hill to die on. One of our sons wanted to dye his hair purple. 'We'll get back to you,' we said. Now what? We reasoned there would be other things that would require a firm and unwavering 'no' – like a bone through his nose or him joining the Ku-Klux Klan. Was this request also of that order? Or could we 'lose' this one in order to have something in reserve to win the battles we believed really mattered?

In the end our son had a shock. 'OK,' his mum said. 'I'll get the dye.' And she did the deed that very evening. The fact that the outcome was a dull auburn and nothing to ever turn a head or attract a glance only made the decision even more palatable. However, the principle holds true. Do you really need to fight over this one? Or is there a more important hill on the horizon on which you need to fight to the death?

Don't deprive as punishment. Now that society has generally moved on from the concept of whacking kids whenever they step out of line, the struggle is to find a workable alternative. The most obvious is to take away privileges. However, child care specialists tell us the only real outcome of doing so is to create resentment.

Top Tip: *Don't use deprivation as a punishment as it only breeds resentment.*

I've always thought that a far better way forward seems to be giving them jobs to do and responsibilities to fulfil as a punishment. If you do face no alternative other than to deprive, the smart thing is to reach an agreement on the terms by which they can have the loss reinstated. In this way you give them hope and an incentive to improve.

When it comes to the practical side of discipline, make sure you:

- *Never nag.* Say it once – or perhaps twice – and stick to it.
- *Never try to sort it out while the child's still mad.* Reason needs a calm environment.
- *Never say what you don't mean.* 'Your mother and I hate you' is not a helpful phrase!
- *Never threaten what you can't carry out.* Two hundred miles from home and under canvas, the threat 'OK, we're going home' lacks reality.
- *Never give in to blackmail.* If they get away with it once you are done for!
- *Never depend totally on either bribes or punishments.* Rewards and recognition for good behaviour are a more effective way to put you in the driving seat.
- *Never impose without involving them in the process.* Help them see the situation through your eyes and to contribute

to the solution. But not if they are only four years old!

- *Never underestimate their intelligence.* Older children may well be able to think through the issues more than you assume.

In contrast, be sure to –

- *Always be reasonable and consistent.* Children have a deep-seated and over-tuned sense of what's fair and get confused with boundaries and expectations that shift with time and circumstances.
- *Always behave like an adult.* There is only ever room for one child in an argument so make sure it's never you.
- *Always explain.* 'Because I say so' didn't work for you as a child and the world has not changed. And it offers no hope for the future.
- *Always look for opportunities to praise and reward good behaviour.* Praise is the greatest motivator a child can receive to prompt them to achieve more of the same.
- *Always be consistent, even in public.* No matter how embarrassing it may be for you, if you give way they will have trained you to allow it to happen again.
- *Always hear them out.* If they have a viewpoint let them express it, don't interrupt. And make sure they know you have understood what they have said.
- *Always* keep the door to the relationship open. Always provide a way back.

Get Help

You are not alone in being a dad. There are some excellent resources and organisations to help you make the very most of it. Four worthy of a particular mention, perhaps, are:

- *Dads and Lads* – locally based projects run jointly by the YMCA and Care for the Family for father and sons, mentors and boys. They offer a unique opportunity to get together with other fathers and sons for a game of football and other activities.
- *The Parentalk Parenting Course* – a video-based resource, which gives groups of mums and dads the chance to get together informally, to talk about their experiences and, together, to discover principles for parenthood.
- *Fathers Direct* – an information resource organisation with a highly practical website.

- *Families Need Fathers* – they are chiefly concerned with the problems of maintaining a child's relationship with both parents during and after family breakdown. If you want to know your rights or find advice and information on how to stay involved with your children and share parenting responsibilities with your children's mother, this is a good place to look.

You'll find further details about these and many other organisations, resources and initiatives at the back of this book.

Ten Things a Dad Never Expects to Hear

1. Are these your socks?
2. Would you like me to clean up my room?
3. I think you ought to know I broke it.
4. Are there any more sprouts?
5. I don't need that much pocket money.
6. You look cool in that outfit.
7. Do we have any Beethoven CDs?
8. Should I brush my sister's hair?
9. What else would you like me to do?
10. Let him choose first.

Let Go

I remember watching a nature film of a blackbird pushing her chicks out of the nest for the first time. She did so believing all she had done up until that point would result in them taking to the air instead of crashing to the ground. Being a dad is really all about the same thing – slowly equipping your child to fly and learning to let them go. There has to come a time when each child becomes big enough and smart enough to begin to make choices for themselves – to begin to fly under their own power.

Every dad's job is to prepare their child for that moment of take-off by loving them, training them, disciplining them and leading by example. And giving them 'test runs' in making choices on their own. Then we trust they will fly according to the radar of the values we have instilled in them and the choices we would make were we in their place.

As they take to the sky, it puts a smile on a father's face. Trust me!

 Top Tip: *Never let a child wearing Superman pyjamas sleep in the top bunk.*

The Last Word

What Would Our Kids Tell Us about Being a Dad?

How does all this advice look to those on the receiving end – the kids we want to be good dads to? I took the risk of asking my five for their feedback – and so giving them the last word. What sticks in their memory from their childhood? And what will they do if and when they are parents themselves?

To my great relief, their feedback underlines this book's core messages. But first, the extra good news. None of these now-almost-mature adults wanted to shine their spotlight on anything negative about my fathering, even though there is plenty I could point to. My excessive discipline of our first, for example. Or often an over-commitment to my work, or the times I jumped to the wrong conclusions. Or my tendency to be negative when my children actually deserve praise. In fact, the more I think about it, the longer the list seems to get!

It seems even though I've often got it wrong, the damage

has been by no means permanent. Perhaps they have some-how picked up that I've been doing my best but, anyway, what a stress-buster!

As to what 'made' their childhood for them, two great themes stick out. The first is 'being there'. The second is the element of 'surprise'.

Being there. They wanted me to know how special were our family holidays which – to keep cost to a minimum – usually involved long journeys to the South of France, with the seven of us packed in the car. Aran told me, 'These journeys weren't always the best of fun, until we played the "look out" game. You would choose five objects we would have to spot outside the car. They always seemed to be a blue van, any two animals, a car with its bonnet up, a police car – and a man having a "tinkle" by the side of the road.'

Isn't that great? The long journey was the only way we could afford to get a family our size to the sun. And the greatest memory didn't cost a penny – just some imagina-tion.

What completed the picture – and again at no cost – was 'doing things as a family on the beach, such as body-board-ing, playing bowls and cricket – and of course you would always win.' Ouch! That's the problem with my competitive personality.

The issue of 'being there' so far as my daughter Xanna is concerned is very different. She highlights the time at second-ary school when she was being bullied by a member of staff, and the head teacher was more concerned to protect the school than her pupil. It was a difficult time for our family that absorbed hours of my time and emotional energy. Xanna told me, 'What I remember most was that you were there for me and didn't let me down. I trusted you, and you stood by me through thick and thin. You showed that your love was unconditional!'

Surprise. Of all the incidents Kristen – my eldest son – could have drawn on, the one he chose is one I had all but forgotten. As a total surprise, I bought him his first bike and took it with me when picking him up from playgroup. He remembers, 'I refused to believe it was mine! I couldn't believe someone could love me that much to give me a bike!'

For Zac, son number four, the story is similar. From the age of twelve he'd wanted to learn to play the drums. Knowing our kids, we set the rules – take lessons at school and if you are still working at it a year later we will try to get you a drum kit. To our surprise he knuckled down.

Christmas came several months before the deadline and so we struck. I found what was needed in *Loot* and hid the kit with a neighbour – who smuggled it into Zac's bedroom while we were all at church on Christmas morning. The climax came when Rosemary's feigned angry voice summoned him to his room in fear he was about to be bawled out for its usual mess. Instead, as Zac came innocently through the door we were there – and so was his to-be-treasured drum kit. The photographs say it all.

What Would They Do?

Just a few key words and phrases surfaced as the result of being asked, 'What would you do as a parent?'

In their own words they would:

- 'Make a special family time, like Sunday meals together.'
- 'Make a big effort over Christmas – opening presents together, going to church together, eating turkey.'
- 'Be there for my children – all the time, through thick and thin.'
- 'Be fair and always listen to their point of view, before telling them the way it really is!'
- 'Tell them that I love them at every opportunity.'

Joel summed it up, 'It's important that kids know how special they are to their parents. My parents have always told me, and this has always helped me know that no matter what I do or say my parents will be there for me with open arms. I want my kids to feel like that too.'

A Little Bonus

The most satisfying thing of all from the feedback I received is quite simple – but to me it's the greatest outcome any dad could wish for. They told me, 'You instilled morals and fairness into me.' And, 'You introduced me to God, and the way to live my life with him. Without that I would be empty.'

What a privilege for a dad. And what a reward after the years of hard work, wonderful joy, constant worry, endless mistakes, frequent arguments, countless apologies, buckets of tears and bags of laughter.

Definitions for Dads

★ *Full name* – what you call your child when you're mad at them.
★ *Grandparents* – the people who think your children are wonderful even though they're not sure you're raising them right.
★ *Teenager* – someone who knows more today than they will ever know in the future.
★ *Independent* – how we want out children to be as long as they do everything we say.
★ *Ow!* – the first word spoken by children with older siblings.
★ *Show-off* – a child who is more talented than yours.

Sometimes You'll Look Good and Not Deserve It

Finally, there are times you will score points far beyond those you deserve. For example, Joel has me down as 'his hero' – but then he's probably after something. As an example he cites 'the time on holiday when we [I must point out here – they!] locked ourselves out of our apartment'. His memory is of being in the swimming pool and looking up at someone

153

on 'at least the fifteenth floor' climbing between balconies to get into our room.

He continues, 'Everyone in the pool area stopped to watch. It didn't take me long to realise it was my dad trying to recover the keys. I was so proud he was the centre of the attention and so brave just for a set of keys.'

However, *my* memory is that the balcony was only a couple of floors up and I much preferred a bit of climbing to sleeping outside for the rest of the week!

Meanwhile, Aran recalls his very best memory as a child as when he won the 'best improved pupil' prize at his junior school. To him it was a huge achievement having come through a period of considerable problems that ended with his desk being moved to outside the headmaster's office! The turnaround came when we discovered he had been nigh on deaf for much of the troubled time and had been working out his frustrations.

Aran's great memory was me seeing him pick up the cup in the school assembly. And my beaming face as I took photographs of him with the cup afterwards. The only thing is, I wasn't there. It was his mother. Which goes to show, if you hang in you can even get credit from your kids for things you didn't do. Now that can't be a bad thing!

One last word. Don't let anything I've just said leave you with the false impression that being a dad, for me, is now somehow a thing of the past. Our kids may be grown up, most now live away from home – one of them is even married – but Rosemary and I are still very much their parents. Despite our failings, we remain anchors in their lives – especially, I've noticed, when the sea gets choppy and the storms rage. In the end, being a dad is a job for life, not a passing vocation. However old your children are, wherever they live, whatever they do, they still need you – the privilege and the responsibility continues. So, as for me, I'm looking forward to the next chapter!

Notes

1. *Why Men Don't Listen and Women Can't Read Maps*, Allan and Barbara Pease, PTI, ISBN 0-646-34917-1, page 30.
2. Taken from a report 'The Fragile Male' by Dr Sebastian Krarmer to the Parent Child 2000 conference.
3. Research – *Girlstalk*, Adrienne Katz, 1996; and *'Can-Do' Girls: A Barometer of Change*, Anne McCoy and Ann Buchanan, 1997.
4. Research – *Girlstalk*, Katz; and *'Can-Do' Girls*, McCoy and Buchanan.
5. *Opinion Research Business*, May 2000.
6. *Social Trends* 28, 29, 74, 87, 88, 89, ONS The Stationery Office.
7. Research by Dr Robert Frank, who interviewed 368 home-dad families for a study at Loyola University, Illinois.

Further Information

Organisations

Parentalk
PO Box 23142
London SE1 OZT

Tel: 0700 2000 500
Fax: 020 7450 9060
e-mail: info@parentalk.co.uk
Web site: www.parentalk.co.uk

Provides a range of resources and services designed to inspire parents to enjoy parenthood.

Dads & Lads
Dirk Uitterdijk
Andy Howie
YMCA England and National Dads & Lads project
Dee Bridge House
25–27 Lower Bridge Street
Chester CH1 1RS

Tel: 01244 403090
e-mail: dirk@parenting.ymca.org.uk
ahowie@themail.co.uk

Locally based projects run jointly by YMCA and Care for the Family for fathers and sons, mentors and boys. They offer a unique opportunity to get together with other fathers and sons for a game of football and other activities. To find out where your nerest Dads & Lads project is based or to get help starting a new one, please contact Dirk Uitterdijk at the above address.

Care for the Family
Garth House, Leon Avenue
Cardiff CF4 7RG

Tel: 029 2081 0800
Fax: 029 2081 4089
e-mail: care.for.the.family@cff.org.uk
Web site: www.care-for-the-family.org.uk

Providing support for families through seminars, resources and special projects.

Fathers Direct
Tamarisk House
37 The Tele Village
Crickhowell
Powys NP8 1BP

Tel: 01873 810515
Web site: www.fathersdirect.com

Information resource for fathers.

Families Need Fathers
134 Curtain Road
London EC2A 3AR

Tel: 0207 613 5060
Web site: www.fnf.org.uk

Provides information and support to parents. Families Need Fathers is chiefly concerned with the problems of maintaining a child's relationship with both parents during the after family breakdown.

Gingerbread
16–17 Clerkenwell Close
London EC1R 0AA

Tel: 020 7336 8183
Fax: 020 7336 8185
e-mail: office@gingerbread.org.uk
Web site: www.gingerbread.org.uk

Provides day-to-day support and practical help for lone parents.

Kidscape
2 Grosvenor Gardens
London SW1W 0DH

Tel: 020 77330 3300
Fax: 020 77330 7081
e-mail: info@kidscape.org.uk
Web site: www.kidscape.org.uk

Works to prevent the abuse of children through education programmes involving parents and teachers, providing a range of resources. Also runs a bullying helpline.

National Council for One Parent Families
255 Kentish Town Road
London NW5 2LX

Lone Parent Line: 0800 018 5026
Maintenance & Money Line: 020 7428 5424
(Mon & Fri 10.30 a.m.–1.30 p.m.; Wed 3–6 p.m.)

Information service for lone parents.

National Drugs Helpline
Healthwise Helplines Limited
First Floor
Cavern Court
8 Matthew Street
Liverpool L2 6RE

Tel: 0800 77 66 00

Free helpline offering confidential advice. Can also send out free leaflets and answer any queries callers might have.

Positive Parenting Publications
1st Floor, 2A South Street
Gosport PO12 1ES

Tel: 01705 528787
Fax: 01705 501111
e-mail: info@parenting.org.uk
Web site: www.parenting.org.uk

Aims to prepare people for the role of parenting by helping parents, those about to become parents and also those who lead parenting groups.

Parentline Plus
520 Highgate Studios
53–76 Highgate Road
Kentish Town
London NW5 1TL

Helpline: 0808 800 2222
Fax: 020 7284 5501
e-mail: centraloffice@parentline plus.org.uk
Web site: www.parentlineplus.org. uk

Provides freephone helpline called Parentline and courses for parents via the Parent Network Service. For all information call the Parentline freephone number on 0808 800 2222.

National Family and Parenting Institute
430 Highgate Studios
53–79 Highgate Road
London NW5 1TL

Tel: 020 7424 3460
Fax: 020 7485 3590
e-mail: info@nfpi.org
Web site: www.nfpi.org

An independent charity set up to provide a strong national focus on parenting and families in the 21st century.

Relate: National Marriage Guidance
National Headquarters
Herbert Gray College
Little Church Street
Rugby, Warwickshire CV21 3AP

Tel: 01788 573241
Fax: 01788 535007
e-mail: enquiries@national.relate. org.uk
Web site: www.relate.org.uk

NSPCC
NSPCC National Centre
42 Curtain Road
London EC2A 3NH

Helpline: 0800 800 500
Tel: 020 7825 2500
Fax: 020 7825 2525
Web site: www.nspcc.org.uk

Aims to prevent child abuse and neglect in all its forms and gives practical help to families with children at risk.

The NSPCC also produces leaf-

161

The Parentalk Guide to Being a Dad

lets with information and advice on positive parenting – for more information phone 020 7825 2500.

Dads Web sites

Mums and Dads
www.parentalk.co.uk
A lively upbeat site, exclusively for parents, packed with fun ideas, practical and expert advice and some great tips about making the most of being a mum or dad.

Stay at home dads
www.slowlane.com (US site)
Aims to help dads connect with each other in their local areas.

Single dads
www.scfn.org (US site)
Supports fathers who bring their children up alone.

National Fatherhood Institute
www.fatherhood.org (US site)
Promoting responsible fatherhood.

Fatherhood magazine
www.fathermag.com (US site)
Online magazine for men with families.

For expectant mums and dads - and beyond
www.b4baby.com
Information and advice on pre-conception, pregnancy, babies and parenting plus online shopping.

For mums and dads!
www.ukmums.co.uk &
www.ukdads.co.uk
Information about pre-conception, pregnancy, labour, birth, babies and toddlers.

From conception through to birth
www.bbc.co.uk/health/parenting
A lively upbeat site, exclusively for parents, packed with fun ideas, practical and expert advice and some great tips about making the most of being a mum or dad.

Publications

The Sixty Minute Father, Rob Parsons, Hodder & Stoughton
How to Succeed as a Parent, Steve Chalke, Hodder & Stoughton
Sex Matters, Steve Chalke and Nick Page, Hodder & Stoughton
Positive Parenting: Raising Children with Self-Esteem, E. Hartley-Brewer, Mandarin
Raising Boys, Steve Biddulph, Thorsons
The Secret of Happy Children, Steve Biddulph, Thorsons
Families and How to Survive Them, Skinner and Cleese, Vermilion
Stress Free Parenting, Dr David Haslam, Vermilion

Parenting Courses

- **Parentalk Parenting Course**
  A new parenting course designed to give parents the opportunity to share their experiences, learn from each other and discover some principles of parenting.
  Parentalk, PO Box 23142, London SE1 0ZT
  For more information phone 0700 2000 500
  e-mail: info@parentalk.co.uk
  Web site: www.parentalk.co.uk / www.parentalkatwork.co.uk

- **Parent Network**
  Operates through self-help groups run by parents for parents known as Parent-Link. The groups are mostly run for 2 or more hours, over 13 weekly sessions.
  For more information call **Parentline Plus** on 0808 800 2222.

- **Positive Parenting**
  Publishes a range of low cost, easy to read, common sense resource materials which provide help, information and advice. Responsible for running a range of parenting courses across the UK. For more information phone 023 9252 8787.

The **Paren**talk Parenting Course

Helping you to be a Better Parent

Being a parent is not easy. **Parentalk** is a new, video-led, parenting course designed to give groups of parents the opportunity to share their experiences, learn from each other and discover some principles of parenting. It is suitable for anyone who is a parent or is planning to become a parent.

The Parentalk Parenting Course features:

Steve Chalke – TV Presenter; author on parenting and family issues; father of four and **Parentalk** Founder.

Rob Parsons – author of *The Sixty Minute Father*; regular TV and radio contributor; and Executive Director of Care for the Family.

Dr Caroline Dickinson – inner city-based GP and specialist in obstetrics, gynaecology and paediatrics.

Kate Robbins – well-known actress and comedienne.

Each **Parentalk** session is packed with group activities and discussion starters.

Made up of eight sessions, the **Parentalk** Parenting Course is easy to use and includes everything you need to host a group of up to ten parents.

Each Parentalk Course Pack contains:
- A Parentalk Video
- Extensive, easy to use, group leader's guide
- Ten copies of the full-colour course material for members
- Photocopiable sheets/OHP masters

Price £49.95

Additional participant materials are available so that the course can be run again and again.

To order your copy, or to find out more, please contact:

Parentalk

PO Box 23142, London SE1 0ZT
Tel: 020 7450 9072 *or* 020 7450 9073
Fax: 020 7450 9060
e-mail: info@parentalk.co.uk